THE GOSPEL OF THOMAS

THE ACTS OF THOMAS

THE BOOK OF THOMAS THE CONTENDER

British Library Cataloguing in Publication Data

A catalogue record for this book is available from the British
Library

ISBN-13: 978-1-908388-04-9

Printed and bound in Great Britain by Lightning Souce UK Ltd., 6
Precedent Drive, Rooksley, Milton Keynes MK13 8PR.

Cover Illustration: Icon of 'Antipascha'

CONTENTS

THE GOSPEL
OF
THOMAS

Thomas O. Lambdin (translator: Coptic version)
B.P Grenfell & A.S. Hunt, and Bentley Layton
(translators:Greek Fragments)

Editorial Symbols

This edition follows the Nag Hammadi Library standard for typographical symbols. Text within:

[square brackets]   = a portion of damaged manuscript reconstructed by the translators;

(parentheses)   = comments/text added for clarification;

<pointed brackets>   = a original scribal error corrected by the translator;

{braces}   = superfluous text added by the scribe.

I

THE COPTIC GOSPEL OF THOMAS

P)
These are the secret sayings which the living Jesus spoke and which Didymos Judas Thomas wrote down.

1) And He said, "Whoever finds the interpretation of these sayings will not experience death."

2) Jesus said, "Let him who seeks continue seeking until he finds. When he finds, he will become troubled. When he becomes troubled, he will be astonished, and he will rule over the All."

3) Jesus said, "If those who lead you say, 'See, the Kingdom is in the sky,' then the birds of the sky will precede you. If they say to you, 'It is in the sea,' then the fish will precede you. Rather, the Kingdom is inside of you, and it is outside of you. When you come to know yourselves, then you will become known, and you will realize that it is you who are the sons of the living Father. But if you will not know yourselves, you dwell in poverty and it is you who are that poverty."

4) Jesus said, "The man old in days will not hesitate to ask a small child seven days old about the place of life, and he will live. For many who are first will become last, and they will become one and the same."

5) Jesus said, "Recognize what is in your sight, and that which is hidden from you will become plain to you. For there is nothing hidden which will not become manifest."

6) His disciples questioned Him and said to Him, "Do you want us to fast? How shall we pray? Shall we give alms? What diet shall we observe?" Jesus said, "Do not tell lies, and do not do what you hate, for all things are plain in the sight of Heaven. For nothing hidden will not become manifest, and nothing covered will remain without being uncovered."

7) Jesus said, "Blessed is the lion which becomes man when consumed by man; and cursed is the man whom the lion consumes, and the lion becomes man."

8) And He said, "The Kingdom is like a wise fisherman who cast his net into the sea and drew it up from the sea full of small fish. Among them the wise fisherman found a fine large fish. He threw all the small fish back into the sea and chose the large fish without difficulty. Whoever has ears to hear, let him hear."

9) Jesus said, "Now the sower went out, took a handful (of seeds), and scattered them. Some fell on the road; the birds came and gathered them up. Others fell on the rock, did not take root in the soil, and did not produce ears. And others fell on thorns; they choked the seed(s) and worms ate them. And others fell on the good soil and produced good fruit: it bore sixty per measure and a hundred and twenty per measure."

10) Jesus said, "I have cast fire upon the world, and see, I am guarding it until it blazes."

11) Jesus said, "This heaven will pass away, and the one above it will pass away. The dead are not alive, and the living will not die. In the days when you consumed what is dead, you made it what is alive. When you come to dwell in the light, what will you do? On the day when you were one you became two. But when you become two, what will you do?"

12) The disciples said to Jesus, "We know that You will depart from us. Who is to be our leader?" Jesus said to them, "Wherever you are, you are to go to James the righteous, for whose sake heaven and earth came into being."

13) Jesus said to His disciples, "Compare me to someone and tell Me whom I am like." Simon Peter said to Him, "You are like a righteous angel." Matthew said to Him, "You are like a wise philosopher." Thomas said to Him, "Master, my mouth is wholly incapable of saying whom You are like." Jesus said, "I am not your master. Because you have drunk, you have become intoxicated by the bubbling spring which I have measured out." And He took him and withdrew and told him three things. When

Thomas returned to his companions, they asked him, "What did Jesus say to you?" Thomas said to them, "If I tell you one of the things which he told me, you will pick up stones and throw them at me; a fire will come out of the stones and burn you up."

14) Jesus said to them, "If you fast, you will give rise to sin for yourselves; and if you pray, you will be condemned; and if you give alms, you will do harm to your spirits. When you go into any land and walk about in the districts, if they receive you, eat what they will set before you, and heal the sick among them. For what goes into your mouth will not defile you, but that which issues from your mouth - it is that which will defile you."

15) Jesus said, "When you see one who was not born of woman, prostrate yourselves on your faces and worship him. That one is your Father."

16) Jesus said, "Men think, perhaps, that it is peace which I have come to cast upon the world. They do not know that it is dissension which I have come to cast upon the earth: fire, sword, and war. For there will be five in a house: three will be against two, and two against three, the father against the son, and the son against the father. And they will stand solitary."

17) Jesus said, "I shall give you what no eye has seen and what no ear has heard and what no hand has touched and what has never occurred to the human mind."

18) The disciples said to Jesus, "Tell us how our end will be." Jesus said, "Have you discovered, then, the beginning, that you look for the end? For where the beginning is, there will the end be. Blessed is he who will take his place in the beginning; he will know the end and will not experience death."

19) Jesus said, "Blessed is he who came into being before he came into being. If you become My disciples and listen to My words, these stones will minister to you. For there are five trees for you in Paradise which remain undisturbed summer and winter and whose leaves do not fall. Whoever becomes acquainted with them will not experience death."

20) The disciples said to Jesus, "Tell us what the Kingdom of Heaven is like." He said to them, "It is like a mustard seed, the smallest of all seeds. But when it falls on tilled soil, it produces a great plant and becomes a shelter for birds of the sky."

21) Mary said to Jesus, "Whom are Your disciples like?" He said, "They are like children who have settled in a field which is not theirs. When the owners of the field come, they will say, 'Let us have back our field.' They (will) undress in their presence in order to let them have back their field and give it back to them. Therefore I say to you, if the owner of a house knows that the thief is coming, he will begin his vigil before he comes and will not let him into his house of his domain to carry away his goods. You, then, be on your guard against the world. Arm yourselves with great strength lest the robbers find a way to come to you, for the difficulty which you expect will (surely) materialize. Let there be among you a man of understanding. When the grain ripened, he came quickly with his sickle in his hand and reaped it. Whoever has ears to hear, let him hear."

22) Jesus saw infants being suckled. He said to His disciples, "These infants being suckled are like those who enter the Kingdom." They said to Him, "Shall we then, as children, enter the Kingdom?" Jesus said to them, "When you make the two one, and when you make the inside like the outside and the outside like the inside, and the above like the below, and when you make the male and the female one and the same, so that the male not be male nor the female female; and when you fashion eyes in the place of an eye, and a hand in place of a hand, and a foot in place of a foot, and a likeness in place of a likeness; then will you enter [the Kingdom]."

23) Jesus said, "I shall choose you, one out of a thousand, and two out of ten thousand, and they shall stand as a single one."

24) His disciples said to Him, "Show us the place where You are, since it is necessary for us to seek it." He said to them, "Whoever has ears, let him hear. There is light within a man of light, and he (or "it") lights up the whole world. If he (or "it") does not shine, he (or "it") is darkness."

25) Jesus said, "Love your brother like your soul, guard him like the pupil of your eye."

26) Jesus said, "You see the mote in your brothers eye, but you do not see the beam in your own eye. When you cast the beam out of your own eye, then you will see clearly to cast the mote from your brother's eye."

27) <Jesus said,> "If you do not fast as regards the world, you will not find the Kingdom. If you do not observe the Sabbath as a Sabbath, you will not see the Father."

28) Jesus said, "I took my place in the midst of the world, and I appeared to them in the flesh. I found all of them intoxicated; I found none of them thirsty. And My soul became afflicted for the sons of men, because they are blind in their hearts and do not have sight; for empty they came into the world, and empty too they seek to leave the world. But for the moment they are intoxicated. When they shake off their wine, then they will repent."

29) Jesus said, "If the flesh came into being because of spirit, it is a wonder. But if spirit came into being because of the body, it is a wonder of wonders. Indeed, I am amazed at how this great wealth has made its home in this poverty."

30) Jesus said, "Where there are three gods, they are gods. Where there are two or one, I am with him."

31) Jesus said, "No prophet is accepted in his own village; no physician heals those who know him."

32) Jesus said, "A city being built on a high mountain and fortified cannot fall, nor can it be hidden."

33) Jesus said, "Preach from your housetops that which you will hear in your ear {(and) in the other ear}. For no one lights a lamp and puts it under a bushel, nor does he put it in a hidden place, but rather he sets it on a lampstand so that everyone who enters and leaves will see its light."

34) Jesus said, "If a blind man leads a blind man, they will both fall into a pit."

35) Jesus said, "It is not possible for anyone to enter the house of a strong man and take it by force unless he binds his hands; then he will (be able to) ransack his house."

36) Jesus said, "Do not be concerned from morning until evening and from evening until morning about what you will wear."

37) His disciples said, "When will You become revealed to us and when shall we see You?" Jesus said, "When you disrobe without being ashamed and take up your garments and place them under your feet like little children and tread on them, then [will you see] the Son of the Living One, and you will not be afraid"

38) Jesus said, "Many times have you desired to hear these words which I am saying to you, and you have no one else to hear them from. There will be days when you look for Me and will not find Me."

39) Jesus said, "The Pharisees and the scribes have taken the keys of Knowledge and hidden them. They themselves have not entered, nor have they allowed to enter those who wish to. You, however, be as wise as serpents and as innocent as doves."

40) Jesus said, "A grapevine has been planted outside of the Father, but being unsound, it will be pulled up by its roots and destroyed."

41) Jesus said, "Whoever has something in his hand will receive more, and whoever has nothing will be deprived of even the little he has."

42) Jesus said, "Become passers-by."

43) His disciples said to him, "Who are You, that You should say these things to us?" <Jesus said to them,> "You do not realize who I am from what I say to you, but you have become like the Jews, for they (either) love the tree and hate its fruit or love the fruit and hate the tree."

44) Jesus said, "Whoever blasphemes against the Father will be forgiven, and whoever blasphemes against the Son will be forgiven, but whoever blasphemes against the Holy Spirit will not be forgiven either on earth or in heaven."

45) Jesus said, "Grapes are not harvested from thorns, nor are figs gathered from thistles, for they do not produce fruit. A good man brings forth good from his storehouse; an evil man brings forth evil things from his evil storehouse, which is in his heart, and says evil things. For out of the abundance of the heart he brings forth evil things."

46) Jesus said, "Among those born of women, from Adam until John the Baptist, there is no one so superior to John the Baptist that his eyes should not be lowered (before him). Yet I have said whichever one of you comes to be a child will be acquainted with the Kingdom and will become superior to John."

47) Jesus said, "It is impossible for a man to mount two horses or to stretch two bows. And it is impossible for a servant to serve two masters; otherwise he will honor the one and treat the other contemptuously. No man drinks old wine and immediately desires to drink new wine. And new wine is not put into old wineskins, lest they burst; nor is old wine put into a new wineskin, lest it spoil it. An old patch is not sewn onto a new garment, because a tear would result."

48) Jesus said, "If two make peace with each other in this one house, they will say to the mountain, 'Move Away,' and it will move away."

49) Jesus said, "Blessed are the solitary and elect, for you will find the Kingdom. For you are from it, and to it you will return."

50) Jesus said, "If they say to you, 'Where did you come from?', say to them, 'We came from the light, the place where the light came into being on its own accord and established [itself] and became manifest through their image.' If they say to you, 'Is it you?', say, 'We are its children, we are the elect of the Living Father.' If they ask you, 'What is the sign of your father in you?', say to them, 'It is movement and repose.'"

51) His disciples said to Him, "When will the repose of the dead come about, and when will the new world come?" He said to them, "What you look forward to has already come, but you do not recognize it."

52) His disciples said to Him, "Twenty-four prophets spoke in Israel, and all of them spoke in You." He said to them, "You have omitted the one living in your presence and have spoken (only) of the dead."

53) His disciples said to Him, "Is circumcision beneficial or not?" He said to them, "If it were beneficial, their father would beget them already circumcised from their mother. Rather, the true circumcision in spirit has become completely profitable."

54) Jesus said, "Blessed are the poor, for yours is the Kingdom of Heaven."

55) Jesus said, "Whoever does not hate his father and his mother cannot become a disciple to Me. And whoever does not hate his brothers and sisters and take up his cross in My way will not be worthy of Me."

56) Jesus said, "Whoever has come to understand the world has found (only) a corpse, and whoever has found a corpse is superior to the world."

57) Jesus said, "The Kingdom of the Father is like a man who had [good] seed. His enemy came by night and sowed weeds among the good seed. The man did not allow them to pull up the weeds; he said to them, 'I am afraid that you will go intending to pull up the weeds and pull up the wheat along with them.' For on the day of the harvest the weeds will be plainly visible, and they will be pulled up and burned."

58) Jesus said, "Blessed is the man who has suffered and found life."

59) Jesus said, "Take heed of the Living One while you are alive, lest you die and seek to see Him and be unable to do so."

60) <They saw> a Samaritan carrying a lamb on his way to Judea. He said to his disciples, "(Why does) that man (carry) the lamb around?" They said to him, "So that he may kill it and eat it." He said to them, "While it is alive, he will not eat it, but only when he has killed it and it

has become a corpse." They said to him, "He cannot do so otherwise." He said to them, "You too, look for a place for yourself within the Repose, lest you become a corpse and be eaten."

61) Jesus said, "Two will rest on a bed: the one will die, and other will live." Salome said to him, "Who are You, man, that You, as though from the One, have come up on my couch and eaten from my table?" Jesus said to her, "I am He who exists from the Undivided. I was given some of the things of my Father." <Salome said,> "I am Your disciple." <Jesus said to her,> "Therefore I say, if he is <undivided>, he will be filled with light, but if he is divided, he will be filled with darkness."

62) Jesus said, "It is to those [who are worthy of My] mysteries that I tell My mysteries. Do not let your left hand know what your right hand is doing."

63) Jesus said, "There was a rich man who had much money. He said, 'I shall put my money to use so that I may sow, reap, plant, and fill my storehouse with produce, with the result that I shall lack nothing. Such were his intentions, but that same night he died. Let him who has ears hear."

64) Jesus said, "A man had received visitors. And when he had prepared the dinner, he sent his servant to invite guests. He went to the first one and said to him, "My master invites you.' He said, 'I have claims against some merchants. They are coming to me this evening. I must go and give them my orders. I ask to be excused from the dinner.' He went to another and said, 'My master has invited you.' He said to him, 'I have just bought a house and am required for the day. I shall not have any spare time.' He went to another and said to him, 'My master invites you.' He said to him, 'My friend is going to get married, and I am to prepare the banquet. I shall not be able to come. I ask to be excused from the dinner.' He went to another and said to him, 'My master invites you.' He said to him, 'I have just bought a farm, and I am on my way to collect the rent. I shall not be able to come. I ask to be excused.' The servant returned and said to his master, 'Those whom you invited to the dinner have asked to be excused.' The master said to his servant, 'Go outside to the streets and bring back those whom you happen to meet, so that they may dine.' Businessmen and merchants will not enter the Places of My Father."

65) He said, "There was a good man who owned a vineyard. He leased it to tenant farmers so that they might work it and he might collect the produce from them. He sent his servant so that the tenants might give him the produce of the vineyard. They seized his servant and beat him, all but killing him. The servant went back and told his master. The master said, 'Perhaps <they> did not recognize <him>.' He sent another servant. The tenants beat this one as well. Then the owner sent his son and said, 'Perhaps they will show respect to my son.' Because the tenants knew that it was he who was the heir to the vineyard, they seized him and killed him. Let him who has ears hear."

66) Jesus said, "Show me the stone which the builders have rejected. That one is the cornerstone."

67) Jesus said, "Whoever believes that the All itself is deficient is (himself) completely deficient."

68) Jesus said, "Blessed are you when you are hated and persecuted. Wherever you have been persecuted they will find no Place."

69) Jesus said, "Blessed are they who have been persecuted within themselves. It is they who have truly come to know the Father. Blessed are the hungry, for the belly of him who desires will be filled."

70) Jesus said, "That which you have will save you if you bring it forth from yourselves. That which you do not have within you will kill you if you do not have it within you."

71) Jesus said, "I shall destroy [this] house, and no one will be able to rebuild it."

72) [A man said] to Him, "Tell my brothers to divide my father's possessions with me." He said to him, "O man, who has made Me a divider?" He turned to His disciples and said to them, "I am not a divider, am I?"

73) Jesus said, "The harvest is great but the laborers are few. Beseech

the Lord, therefore, to send out laborers to the harvest."

74) He said, "O Lord, there are many around the drinking trough, but there is nothing in the cistern."

75) Jesus said, "Many are standing at the door, but it is the solitary who will enter the bridal chamber."

76) Jesus said, "The kingdom of the Father is like a merchant who had a consignment of merchandise and who discovered a pearl. That merchant was shrewd. He sold the merchandise and bought the pearl alone for himself. You too, seek his unfailing and enduring treasure where no moth comes near to devour and no worm destroys."

77) Jesus said, "It is I who am the light which is above them all. It is I who am the All. From Me did the All come forth, and unto Me did the All extend. Split a piece of wood, and I am there. Lift up the stone, and you will find Me there."

78) Jesus said, "Why have you come out into the desert? To see a reed shaken by the wind? And to see a man clothed in fine garments like your kings and your great men? Upon them are the fine [garments], and they are unable to discern the truth."

79) A woman from the crowd said to Him, "Blessed are the womb which bore You and the breasts which nourished You." He said to her, "Blessed are those who have heard the word of the Father and have truly kept it. For there will be days when you will say, 'Blessed are the womb which has not conceived and the breasts which have not given milk.'"

80) Jesus said, "He who has recognized the world has found the body, but he who has found the body is superior to the world."

81) Jesus said, "Let him who has grown rich be king, and let him who possesses power renounce it."

82) Jesus said, "He who is near Me is near the fire, and he who is far from Me is far from the Kingdom."

83) Jesus said, "The images are manifest to man, but the light in them remains concealed in the image of the light of the Father. He will become manifest, but his image will remain concealed by his light."

84) Jesus said, "When you see your likeness, you rejoice. But when you see your images which came into being before you, and which neither die not become manifest, how much you will have to bear!"

85) Jesus said, "Adam came into being from a great power and a great wealth, but he did not become worthy of you. For had he been worthy, [he would] not [have experienced] death."

86) Jesus said, "[The foxes have their holes] and the birds have [their] nests, but the Son of Man has no place to lay his head and rest."

87) Jesus said, "Wretched is the body that is dependant upon a body, and wretched is the soul that is dependent on these two."

88) Jesus said, "The angels and the prophets will come to you and give you those things you (already) have. And you too, give them those things which you have, and say to yourselves, 'When will they come and take what is theirs?'"

89) Jesus said, "Why do you wash the outside of the cup? Do you not realize that he who made he inside is the same one who made the outside?"

90) Jesus said, "Come unto me, for My yoke is easy and My lordship is mild, and you will find repose for yourselves."

91) They said to Him, "Tell us who You are so that we may believe in You." He said to them, "You read the face of the sky and of the earth, but you have not recognized the one who is before you, and you do not know how to read this moment."

92) Jesus said, "Seek and you will find. Yet, what you asked Me about in former times and which I did not tell you then, now I do desire to tell,

but you do not enquire after it."

93) <Jesus said,> "Do not give what is holy to dogs, lest they throw them on the dung-heap. Do not throw the pearls to swine, lest they grind it [to bits]."

94) Jesus [said], "He who seeks will find, and [he who knocks] will be let in."

95) [Jesus said,] "If you have money, do not lend it at interest, but give [it] to one from whom you will not get it back."

96) Jesus [said], "The Kingdom of the Father is like a certain woman. She took a little leaven, [concealed] it in some dough, and made it into large loaves. Let him who has ears hear."

97) Jesus said, "The Kingdom of the [Father] is like a certain woman who was carrying a jar full of meal. While she was walking [on] a road, still some distance from home, the handle of the jar broke and the meal emptied out behind her on the road. She did not realize it; she had noticed no accident. When she reached her house, she set the jar down and found it empty."

98) Jesus said, "The Kingdom of the Father is like a certain man who wanted to kill a powerful man. In his own house he drew his sword and stuck it into the wall in order to find out whether his hand could carry through. Then he slew the powerful man."

99) The disciples said to Him, "Your brothers and Your mother are standing outside." He said to them, "Those here who do the will of My Father are My brothers and My mother. It is they who will enter the Kingdom of My Father."

100) They showed Jesus a gold coin and said to Him, "Caesar's men demand taxes from us." He said to them, "Give Caesar what belongs to Caesar, give God what belongs to God, and give Me what is Mine."

101) <Jesus said,> "Whoever does not hate his father and his mother

as I do cannot become a disciple to Me. And whoever does [not] love his father and his mother as I do cannot become a [disciple] to Me. For My mother [gave me falsehood], but [My] true [Mother] gave me life."

102) Jesus said, "Woe to the Pharisees, for they are like a dog sleeping in the manger of oxen, for neither does he eat nor does he let the oxen eat."

103) Jesus said, "Fortunate is the man who knows where the brigands will enter, so that he may get up, muster his domain, and arm himself before they invade."

104) They said [to Jesus], "Come, let us pray today and let us fast." Jesus said, "What is the sin that I have committed, or wherein have I been defeated? But when the bridegroom leaves the bridal chamber, then let them fast and pray."

105) Jesus said, "He who knows the father and the mother will be called the son of a harlot."

106) Jesus said, "When you make the two one, you will become the sons of man, and when you say, 'Mountain, move away,' it will move away."

107) Jesus said, "The Kingdom is like a shepherd who had a hundred sheep. One of them, the largest, went astray. He left the ninety-nine sheep and looked for that one until he found it. When he had gone to such trouble, he said to the sheep, 'I care for you more than the ninety-nine.'"

108) Jesus said, "He who will drink from my mouth will become like Me. I myself shall become he, and the things that are hidden will become revealed to him."

109) Jesus said, "The Kingdom is like a man who had a [hidden] treasure in his field without knowing it. And [after] he died, he left it to his son. The son did not know (about the treasure). He inherited the field and sold [it]. And the one who bought it went plowing and found the treasure. He began to lend money at interest to whomever he wished."

110) Jesus said, "Whoever finds the world and becomes rich, let him renounce the world."

111) Jesus said, "The heavens and the earth will be rolled up in your presence. And one who lives from the Living One will not see death." Does not Jesus say, "Whoever finds himself is superior to the world?"

112) Jesus said, "Woe to the flesh that depends on the soul; woe to the soul that depends on the flesh."

113) His disciples said to Him, "When will the Kingdom come?" <Jesus said,> "It will not come by waiting for it. It will not be a matter of saying 'Here it is' or 'There it is.' Rather, the Kingdom of the Father is spread out upon the earth, and men do not see it."

114) Simon Peter said to Him, "Let Mary leave us, for women are not worthy of Life." Jesus said, "I myself shall lead her in order to make her male, so that she too may become a living spirit resembling you males. For every woman who will make herself male will enter the Kingdom of Heaven."

II

FRAGMENTS OF THE GREEK
GOSPEL OF THOMAS

Several fragments of a Greek version of Thomas were found among the Oxyrhynchys Papyri in the late 19th century. These fragments consist of the preamble, and sayings 1-6, 26-28, 30-32, 36-38, and 39, as well as a saying not found in the Coptic version, which follows 32. These fragments are found on Oxyrhynchus Papyri 1, 654, and 655. Generally, the sayings are essentially the same in both versions. However, the equivalent of saying 30 adds the end of the Coptic version's saying 77. This translation is a combination of those of B.P. Grenfell, and A.S. Hunt and Bentley Layton.

○○

These are the secret sayings which were spoken by Jesus the Living One, and which Judas, who is called Thomas, wrote down"

1) He said to them: "Whoever hears these words shall never taste death."

2) [Jesus said]: "Let him who seeks not cease until he finds, and when he finds he shall wonder; wondering he shall reign, and reigning shall rest."

3) Jesus said, "If those who attract you say, 'See, the Kingdom is in the sky,' then the birds of the sky will precede you. If they say to you, 'It is under the earth,' then the fish of the sea will precede you. Rather, the Kingdom of God is inside of you, and it is outside of you. [Those who] become acquainted with [themselves] will find it; [and when you] become acquainted with yourselves, [you will understand that] it is you who are the sons of the living Father. But if you will not know yourselves, you dwell in poverty and it is you who are that poverty."

4) Jesus said: "Let the old man who is full of days not hesitate to ask the child of seven days about the place of life; then he will live. For many that are first will be last, and last, first, and they will become a single one."

5) Jesus said: "Recognize what is before your face and that which is hidden from the you will be revealed to you. For there is nothing hidden which shall not be made manifest, nor buried which shall not be raised."

6) His disciples asked him and said to him, "How do you want us to fast? And how shall we pray? And how [shall we] give alms? And what kind of diet shall we follow?" Jesus said, "Do not lie, and do not do what you hate, for all things are disclosed before truth. For there is nothing hidden which shall not be shown forth."

27) Jesus said: "Unless you fast to the world, you shall in no way find the Kingdom of God; and unless you sabbatize the Sabbath, you shall not see the Father."

28) Jesus said: "I stood in the midst of the world, and in the flesh I was seen by them, and I found all drunken, and I found none among them thirsty. And my soul grieved over the souls of men, because they are blind in their heart and see not. [...]

30/77) Jesus said: "Where there are [two, they are not] without God, and when there is one alone, [I say,] I am with him. Raise the stone, and there you will find me; cleave the wood, and there I am."

31) Jesus said: "A prophet is not acceptable in his own country, neither does a physician work cures upon those that know him."

32) Jesus said: "A city built on the top of a high hill and fortified can neither fall nor be hid." -) Jesus said: "Thou hearest with one ear, [but the other thou has closed].

36) Jesus said, "Do not worry from dawn to dusk and from dusk to dawn about [what food] you [will] eat, [or] what [clothing] you will wear. [You are much] better than the [lilies], which [neither] card nor

spin. And for your part, what [will you wear] when you have no clothing? Who would add to your stature? It is he who will give you your clothing.

37) His disciples said to him, "When will you be visible to us, and when shall we behold you?" He said, "When you strip naked without being ashamed, and take your garments and put them under your feet like little children and tread upon them, then you will see the child of the Living, and you will not be afraid."

III

Comparison of Thomas Sayings with Canonical Text

Close Parallels

9: Matthew 13:3-8, Mark 4:3-8, Luke 8:5-8
10: Luke 12:49
16: Matthew 10:34-36, Luke 12:51-53
20: Matthew 13:31-32, Mark 4:30-32, Luke13:18-19
26: Matthew 7:3-5, Luke 6:41-42
34: Matthew 15:14, Luke 6:39
35: Matthew 12:29, Mark 3:27, Luke 11:21-22
41: Matthew 25:29, Luke 19:26
45: Matthew 7:16-20, Luke 6:43-46
46: Matthew 11:11, Luke 7:28
54: Matthew 5:3, Luke 6:20
64: Matthew 22:3-9, Luke 14:16-24
65: Matthew 21:33-39, Mark 12:1-8, Luke 20:9-15
66: Matthew 21:42, Mark 12:10, Luke 20:17; Psalm 118:22
73: Matthew 9:37-38, Luke 10:2
86: Matthew 8:20, Luke 9:58
89: Luke 11:39-40
93: Matthew 7:6
94: Matthew 7:7-8, Luke 11:9-10
100: Mark 12:13-17, Luke 20:22-25
103: Matthew 24:43, Luke 12:39
107: Matthew 18:12-13, Luke 15:3-7

Remote Parallels

1: John 8:51 3: Luke 17:21
5: Matthew 10:26, Luke 10:2
8: Matthew 13:47-48
17: 1 Cor 2:9; Isiah 64:4
30: Matthew 18:20
31: Mark 6:4, Luke 4:23-24, John 4:44

32: Matthew 5:14
36: Matthew 6:25, Luke 12:22
40: Matthew 15:13
44: Matthew 12:32, Mark 3:28-29, Luke 12:10
48: Matthew 18:19, Mark 11:23-24
57: Matthew 13:24-30
58: Matthew 11:28
59: John 7:34, John 13:33
63: Luke 12:16-21
68: Matthew 5:11, Luke 6:22
71: Mark 14:58
72: Luke 12:13-15
75: Matthew 22:14
78: Matthew11:7-9, Luke 7:24-26
90: Matthew 11:28-30
95: Luke 6:34-35, Luke 14:12-14
96: Matthew13:33, Luke 13:20-21
99: Matthew 12:46-50, Mark 3:31-35
101: Matthew 10:37, Luke 14:26
109: Matthew 13:44
113: Luke 17:20-21

Multiple Parallels

14b: Luke 10:8-9
14c: Matthew 15:11, Mark7:15
21b: Matthew 24:43, Luke 12:39
21c: Mark 4:26-29
22a: Matthew18:3, Luke 18:17
22b: Matthew 5:29-30, Mark 9:43-48
24a: John 13:36
24b: Matthew 6:22-23, Luke 11:34-36
33a: Matthew 10:27
33b: Matthew 5:15, Mark 4:21, Luke 8:16, Luke 11:33
39a: Luke 11:52
39b: Matthew 10:16
43a: John 8:25
43b: Matthew 7:16-20, Luke 6:43-46(?)

55a: Luke 14:26
55b: Matthew 10:37
62a: Matthew 13:11, Mark 4:11, Luke 8:10
62b: Matthew 6:3
69a: Matthew 5:8 (cf. Thomas saying 68)
69b: Matthew 5:6, Luke6:21
76a: Matthew 13:45-46
76b: Matthew 6:20, Luke12:33
79a: Luke 11:27-28
79b: Luke 23:29
91a: John 9:36
91b: Luke 12:54-56

Non-Canonical Parallels

42: Some strands of Islamic tradition attribute this saying to Jesus.

No Parallels

Sayings, Number:

2	23	51	77	98
4	25	52	80	102
6	27	53	81	104
7	28	56	82	105
11	29	60	84	106
12	37	61	85	108
13	38	67	87	110
15	47	70	88	111
18	49	73	92	112
19	50	74	97	114

THE ACTS
OF
THOMAS

M. R. James (translator)

Introduction

This is the only one of the five primary romances which we possess in its entirety. It is of great length and considerable interest. The Stichometry (see p. 24) gives it only 1,600 lines: this is far too little: it may probably apply only to a portion of the Acts, single episodes of which, in addition to the Martyrdom, may have been current separately. We do, in fact, find some separate miracles in some of the oriental versions.

There is a consensus of opinion among Syriac scholars that our Greek text of these Acts is a version from Syriac. The Syriac original was edited and translated by Wright in his Apocryphal Acts, and older fragments have since been published by Mrs. Lewis (Horae Semiticae IV, 1904. Mythological Acts of the Apostles).

Certain hymns occur in the Syriac which were undoubtedly composed in that language: most notable is the Hymn of the Soul (edited separately by A. A. Bevan, and others) which is not relevant to the context. It has been ascribed to Bardaisan the famous Syrian heretic. Only one Greek MS. of the Acts (the Vallicellian, at Rome, Bonnet's MS. U, of the eleventh century) contains it; it is paraphrased by Nicetas of Thessalonica in his Greek rechauffe of the Acts.

There is, in fact, no room to doubt that the whole text of the Acts, as preserved complete in MS. U and partially in other manuscripts, is a translation from the Syriac. But in the Martyrdom four manuscripts (including a very important Paris copy-Gr. 1510, of eleventh century, and another of ninth century) present a quite different, and superior. text, indubitably superior in one striking point: that whereas Syr. places the great prayer of Thomas in the twelfth Act, some little time before the Martyrdom (ch. 144 sqq.), the four manuscripts place it immediately before, after ch. 167, and this is certainly the proper place for it.

It is, I believe, still arguable (though denied by the Syriacists) that here is a relic of the original Greek text: in other words, the Acts were composed in Greek, and early rendered into Syriac. Becoming scarce or being wholly lost in Greek they were retranslated out of Syriac into Greek. But meanwhile the original Greek of the Martyrdom had survived separately, and we have it here. This was M. Bonnet's view, and it is one which I should like to adopt.

At the very least, we have a better text of the Martyrdom preserved in these four manuscripts than in U and its congeners.

As to other versions. The Latin Passions-one probably by Gregory of Tours- have been much adulterated. We have also Ethiopic versions of some episodes, and there is also an Armenian one of which little use has been made. However, versions are of little account in this case, where we have such comparatively good authorities as the Greek and Syriac for the whole book.

My version is made from the Greek text, (Bonnet, 1903) with an eye on the Syriac as rendered by Wright and by Mrs. Lewis and Bevan.

M. R. James

Important Archive Note:

In the text below, M. R. James uses brackets [ ] and parentheses ( ) to contain notes on lacunae, questionable words, and manuscript versions used in his translation. Bracketed words are often sometimes literal translations of the original text and are not always easily understood.

Acts of the Holy Apostle Thomas

THE FIRST ACT

When he went into India with Abbanes the merchant

At that season all we the apostles were at Jerusalem, Simon which is called Peter and Andrew his brother, James the son of Zebedee and John his brother, Philip and Bartholomew, Thomas and Matthew the publican, James the son of Alphaeus and Simon the Canaanite, and Judas the brother of James: and we divided the regions of the world, that every one of us should go unto the region that fell to him and unto the nation whereunto the Lord sent him.

According to the lot, therefore, India fell unto Judas Thomas, which is also the twin: but he would not go, saying that by reason of the weakness of the flesh he could not travel, and 'I am an Hebrew man; how can I go amongst the Indians and preach the truth?' And as he thus reasoned and spake, the Saviour appeared unto him by night and saith to him: Fear not, Thomas, go thou unto India and preach the word there, for my grace is with thee. But he would not obey, saying: Whither thou wouldest send me, send me, but elsewhere, for unto the Indians I will not go.

2 And while he thus spake and thought, it chanced that there was there a certain merchant come from India whose name was Abbanes, sent from the King Gundaphorus [Gundaphorus is a historical personage who reigned over a part of India in the first century after Christ. His coins bear his name in Greek, as Hyndopheres], and having commandment from him to buy a carpenter and bring him unto him.

Now the Lord seeing him walking in the market-place at noon said unto him: Wouldest thou buy a carpenter? And he said to him: Yea. And the Lord said to him: I have a slave that is a carpenter and I desire to sell him. And so saying he showed him Thomas afar off, and agreed with him for three litrae of silver unstamped, and wrote a deed of sale, saying: I, Jesus, the son of Joseph the carpenter, acknowledge that I have sold my slave, Judas by name, unto thee Abbanes, a merchant of Gundaphorus, king of the Indians. And when the deed was finished, the Saviour took Judas Thomas and led him away to Abbanes the merchant, and when Abbanes saw him he said unto him: Is this thy master? And the apostle said: Yea, he is my Lord. And he said: I have bought thee of him. And thy apostle held his peace.

3 And on the day following the apostle arose early, and having prayed and besought the Lord he said: I will go whither thou wilt, Lord Jesus: thy will be done. And he departed unto Abbanes the merchant, taking with him nothing at all save only his price. For the Lord had given it unto him, saying: Let thy price also be with thee, together with my grace, wheresoever thou goest.

And the apostle found Abbanes carrying his baggage on board the ship; so he also began to carry it aboard with him. And when they were embarked in the ship and were set down Abbanes questioned the apostle, saying: What craftsmanship knowest thou? And he said: In wood I can make ploughs and yokes and augers (ox-goads, Syr.), and boats and oars for boats and masts and pulleys; and in stone, pillars and temples and court-houses for kings. And Abbanes the merchant said to him: Yea, it is of such a workman that we have need. They began then to sail homeward; and they had a favourable wind, and sailed prosperously till they reached Andrapolis, a royal city.

4 And they left the ship and entered into the city, and lo, there were noises of flutes and water-organs, and trumpets sounded about them; and the apostle inquired, saying: What is this festival that is in this city? And they that were there said to him: Thee also have the gods brought to make merry in this city. For the king hath an only daughter, and now he giveth her in marriage unto an husband: this rejoicing, therefore, and assembly of the wedding to-day is the festival which thou hast seen. And the king hath sent heralds to proclaim everywhere that all should come to the marriage, rich and poor, bond and free, strangers and citizens: and if any refuse and come not to the marriage he shall answer for it unto the king. And Abbanes hearing that, said to the apostle: Let us also go, lest we offend the king, especially seeing we are strangers. And he said: Let us go.

And after they had put up in the inn and rested a little space they went to the marriage; and the apostle seeing them all set down (reclining), laid himself, he also, in the midst, and all looked upon him, as upon a stranger and one come from a foreign land: but Abbanes the merchant, being his master, laid himself in another place.

5 And as they dined and drank, the apostle tasted nothing; so they that were about him said unto him: Wherefore art thou come here, neither eating nor drinking? but he answered them, saying: I am come here for somewhat greater than the food or the drink, and that I may fulfil the king's will. For the heralds proclaim the king's message, and whoso hearkeneth not to the heralds shall be subject to the king's judgement.

So when they had dined and drunken, and garlands and unguents were brought to them, every man took of the unguent, and one anointed his face and another his beard and another other parts of his body; but the apostle anointed the top of his head and smeared a little upon his nostrils, and dropped it into his ears and touched his teeth with it, and carefully anointed the parts about his heart: and the wreath that was brought to him, woven of myrtle and other flowers, he took, and set it on his head, and took a branch of calamus and held it in his hand.

Now the flute-girl, holding her flute in her hand, went about to them all and played, but when she came to the place where the apostle was, she stood over him and played at his head for a long space: now this flute-girl was by race an Hebrew.

6 And as the apostle continued looking on the ground, one of the cup-bearers stretched forth his hand and gave him a buffet; and the apostle lifted up his eyes and looked upon him that smote him and said: My God will forgive thee in the life to come this iniquity, but in this world thou shalt show forth his wonders and even now shall I behold this hand that hath smitten me dragged by dogs. And having so said, he began to sing and to say this song:

The damsel is the daughter of light, in whom consisteth and dwelleth the proud brightness of kings, and the sight of her is delightful, she shineth with beauty and cheer. Her garments are like the flowers of spring, and from them a waft of fragrance is borne; and in the crown of her head the king is established which with his immortal food (ambrosia) nourisheth them that are founded upon him; and in her head is set truth, and with her feet she showeth forth joy. And her mouth is opened, and it becometh her well: thirty and two are they that sing praises to her. Her tongue is like the curtain of the door, which waveth to and fro for them that enter in: her neck is set in the fashion of steps which the first maker hath wrought, and her two hands signify and show, proclaiming the dance of the happy ages, and her fingers point out the gates of the city. Her chamber is bright with light and breatheth forth the odour of balsam and all spices, and giveth out a sweet smell of myrrh and Indian leaf, and within are myrtles strown on the floor, and [GARLANDS] of all manner of odorous flowers, and the door-posts(?) are adorned with freedst.

7 And surrounding her her groomsmen keep her, the number of whom is seven, whom she herself hath chosen. And her bridesmaids are seven, and they dance before her. And twelve in number are they that serve before her and are subject unto her, which have their aim and their look toward the bridegroom, that by the sight of him they may be enlightened; and for ever shall they be with her in that eternal joy, and shall be at that marriage whereto the princes are gathered together and shall attend at that banquet whereof the eternal ones are accounted worthy, and shall put on royal raiment and be clad in bright robes; and in joy and exultation shall they both be and shall glorify the Father of all, whose proud light they have received, and are enlightened by the sight of their lord; whose immortal food they have received, that hath no failing (excrementum, Syr.), and have drunk of the wine that giveth then neither thirst nor desire. And they have glorified and praised with the living spirit, the Father of truth and the mother of wisdom.

8 And when he had sung and ended this song, all that were there present gazed upon him; and he kept silence, and they saw that his likeness was changed, but that which was spoken by him they understood not, forasmuch as he was an Hebrew and that which he spake was said in the Hebrew tongue. But the flute-girl alone heard all of it, for she was by race an Hebrew and she went away from him and played to the rest, but for the most part she gazed and looked upon him, for she loved him well, as a man of her own nation; moreover he was comely to look upon beyond all that were there. And when the flute-girl had played to them all and ended, she sat down over against him, gazing and looking earnestly upon him. But he looked upon no man at all, neither took heed of any but only kept his eyes looking toward the ground, waiting the time when he might depart thence.

But the cup-bearer that had buffeted him went down to the well to draw water; and there chanced to be a lion there, and it slew him and left him Lying in that place, having torn his limbs in pieces, and forthwith dogs seized his members, and among them one black dog holding his right hand in his mouth bare it into the place of the banquet.

9 And all when they saw it were amazed and inquired which of them it was that was missing. And when it became manifest that it was the hand of the cup-bearer which had smitten the apostle, the flute-girl brake her flute and cast it away and went and sat down at the apostle's feet, saying: This is either a god or an apostle of God, for I heard him say in the Hebrew tongue: ' I shall now see the hand that hath smitten me dragged by dogs', which thing ye also have now beheld; for as he said, so hath it come about. And some believed her, and some not.

But when the king heard of it, he came and said to the apostle: Rise up and come with me, and pray for my daughter: for she is mine only-begotten, and to-day I give her in marriage. But the apostle was not willing to go with him, for the Lord was not yet revealed unto him in that place. But the king led him away against his will unto the bride-chamber that he might pray for them.

10 And the apostle stood, and began to pray and to speak thus: My Lord and MY God, that travellest with thy servants, that guidest and correctest them that believe in thee, the refuge and rest of the oppressed, the hope of the poor and ransomer of captives, the physician of the souls that lie sick and saviour of all creation, that givest life unto the world and strengthenest souls; thou knowest things to come, and by our means accomplishest them: thou Lord art he that revealeth hidden mysteries and maketh manifest words that are secret: thou Lord art the planter of the good tree, and of thine hands are all good works engendered: thou Lord art he that art in all things and passest through all, and art set in all thy works and manifested in the working of them all. Jesus Christ, Son of compassion and perfect saviour, Christ, Son of the living God, the undaunted power that hast overthrown the enemy, and the voice that was heard of the rulers, and made all their powers to quake, the ambassador that wast sent from the height and camest down even unto hell, who didst open the doors and bring up thence them that for many ages were shut up in the treasury of darkness, and showedst them the way that leadeth up unto the height: I beseech thee, Lord Jesu, and offer unto thee supplication for these young persons, that thou wouldest do for them the things that shall help them and be expedient and profitable for them. And he laid his hands on them and said: The Lord shall be with you, and left them in that place and departed.

11 And the king desired the groomsmen to depart out of the bride-chamber; and when all were gone out and the doors were shut, the bridegroom lifted up the curtain of the bride-chamber to fetch the bride unto him. And he saw the Lord Jesus bearing the likeness of Judas Thomas and speaking with the bride; even of him that but now had blessed them and gone out from them, the apostle; and he saith unto him: Wentest thou not out in the sight of all? how then art thou found here? But the Lord said to him: I am not Judas which is also called Thomas but I am his brother. And the Lord sat down upon the bed and bade them also sit upon chairs, and began to say unto them:

12 Remember, my children, what my brother spake unto you and what he delivered before you: and know this, that if ye abstain from this foul intercourse, ye become holy temples, pure, being quit of impulses and pains, seen and unseen, and ye will acquire no cares of life or of children, whose end is destruction: and if indeed ye get many children, for their sakes ye become grasping and covetous, stripping orphans and overreaching widows, and by so doing subject yourselves to grievous punishments. For the more part of children become useless oppressed of devils, some openly and some invisibly, for they become either lunatic or half withered or blind or deaf or dumb or paralytic or foolish; and if they be sound, again they will be vain, doing useless or abominable acts, for they will be caught either in adultery or murder or theft or fornication, and by all these will ye be afflicted.

But if ye be persuaded and keep your souls chaste before God, there will come unto you living children whom these blemishes touch not, and ye shall be without care, leading a tranquil life without grief or anxiety, looking to receive that incorruptible and true marriage, and ye shall be therein groomsmen entering into that bride-chamber which is full of immortality and light.

13 And when the young people heard these things, they believed the Lord and gave themselves up unto him, and abstained from foul desire and continued so, passing the night in that place. And the Lord departed from before them, saying thus: The grace of the Lord shall be with you.

And when the morning was come the king came to meet them and furnished a table and brought it in before the bridegroom and the bride. And he found them sitting over against each other and the face of the bride he found unveiled, and the bridegroom was right joyful.

And the mother came unto the bride and said: Why sittest thou so, child, and art not ashamed, but art as if thou hadst lived with thine husband a long season? And her father said: Because of thy great love toward thine husband dost thou not even veil thyself?

14 And the bride answered and said: Verily, father, I am in great love, and I pray my Lord that the love which I have perceived this night may abide with me, and I will ask for that husband of whom I have learned to-day: and therefore I will no more veil myself, because the mirror (veil) of shame is removed from me; and therefore am I no more ashamed or abashed, because the deed of shame and confusion is departed far from me; and that I am not confounded, it is because my astonishment hath not continued with me; and that I am in cheerfulness and joy, it is because the day of my joy hath not been troubled; and that I have set at nought this husband and this marriage that passeth away from before mine eyes, it is because I am joined in another marriage; and that I have had no intercourse with a husband that is temporal, whereof the end is with lasciviousness and bitterness of soul, it is because I am yoked unto a true husband.

15 And while the bride was saying yet more than this, the bridegroom answered and said: I give thee thanks, O Lord, that hast been proclaimed by the stranger, and found in us; who hast removed me far from corruption and sown life in me; who hast rid me of this disease that is hard to be healed and cured and abideth for ever, and hast implanted sober health in me; who hast shown me thyself and revealed unto me all my state wherein I am; who hast redeemed me from falling and led me to that which is better, and set me free from temporal things and made me worthy of those that are immortal and everlasting; that hast made thyself lowly even down to me and my littleness, that thou mayest present me unto thy greatness and unite me unto thyself; who hast not withheld thine own bowels from me that was ready to perish, but hast shown me how to seek myself and know who I was, and who and in what manner I now am, that I may again become that which I was: whom I knew not, but thyself didst seek me out: of whom I was not aware, but thyself hast taken me to thee: whom I have perceived, and now am not able to be unmindful of him: whose love burneth within me, and I cannot speak it as is fit, but that which I am able to say of it is little and scanty, and not fitly proportioned unto his glory: yet he blameth me not that presume to say unto him even that which I know not: for it is because of his love that I say even this much.

16 Now when the king heard these things from the bridegroom and the bride, he rent his clothes and said unto them that stood by him: Go forth

quickly and go about the whole city, and take and bring me that man that is a sorcerer who by ill fortune came unto this city; for with mine own hands I brought him into this house, and I told him to pray over this mine ill-starred daughter; and whoso findeth and bringeth him to me, I will give him whatsoever he asketh of me. They went, therefore and went about seeking him, and found him not; for he had set sail. They went also unto the inn where he had lodged and found there the flute-girl weeping and afflicted because he had not taken her with him. And when they told her the matter that had befallen with the young people she was exceeding glad at hearing it, and put away her grief and said: Now have I also found rest here. And she rose up and went unto them, and was with them a long time, until they had instructed the king also. And many of the brethren also gathered there until they heard the report of the apostle, that he was come unto the cities of India and was teaching there: and they departed and joined themselves unto him.

THE SECOND ACT

Concerning his coming unto the king Gundaphorus

17 Now when the apostle was come into the cities of India with Abbanes the merchant, Abbanes went to salute the king Gundaphorus, and reported to him of the carpenter whom he had brought with him. And the king was glad, and commanded him to come in to him. So when he was come in the king said unto him: What craft understandest thou? The apostle said unto him: The craft of carpentering and of building. The king saith unto him: What craftsmanship, then, knowest thou in wood, and what in stone? The apostle saith: In wood: ploughs, yokes, goads, pulleys, and boats and oars and masts; and in stone: pillars, temples, and court-houses for kings. And the king said: Canst thou build me a palace? And he answered: Yea, I can both build and furnish it; for to this end am I come, to build and to do the work of a carpenter.

18 And the king took him and went out of the city gates and began to speak with him on the way concerning the building of the court-house, and of the foundations, how they should be laid, until they came to the

place wherein he desired that the building should be; and he said: Here will I that the building should be. And the apostle said: Yea, for this place is suitable for the building. But the place was woody and there was much water there. So the king said: Begin to build. But he said: I cannot begin to build now at this season. And the king said: When canst thou begin? And he said: I will begin in the month Dius and finish in Xanthicus. But the king marvelled and said: Every building is builded in summer, and canst thou in this very winter build and make ready a palace? And the apostle said: Thus it must be, and no otherwise is it possible. And the king said: If, then, this seem good to thee, draw me a plan, how the work shall be, because I shall return hither after some long time. And the apostle took a reed and drew, measuring the place; and the doors he set toward the sunrising to look toward the light, and the windows toward the west to the breezes, and the bakehouse he appointed to be toward the south and the aqueduct for the service toward the north. And the king saw it and said to the apostle: Verily thou art a craftsman and it belitteth thee to be a servant of kings. And he left much money with him and departed from him.

19 And from time to time he sent money and provision, and victual for him and the rest of the workmen. But Thomas receiving it all dispensed it, going about the cities and the villages round about, distributing and giving alms to the poor and afflicted, and relieving them, saying: The king knoweth how to obtain recompense fit for kings, but at this time it is needful that the poor should have refreshment.

After these things the king sent an ambassador unto the apostle, and wrote thus: Signify unto me what thou hast done or what I shall send thee, or of what thou hast need. And the apostle sent unto him, saying: The palace (praetorium) is builded and only the roof remaineth. And the king hearing it sent him again gold and silver (lit. unstamped), and wrote unto him: Let the palace be roofed, if it is done. And the apostle said unto the Lord: I thank thee O Lord in all things, that thou didst die for a little space that I might live for ever in thee, and that thou hast sold me that by me thou mightest set free many. And he ceased not to teach and to refresh the afflicted, saying: This hath the Lord dispensed unto you, and he giveth unto every man his food: for he is the nourisher of orphans and steward of the widows, and unto all that are afflicted he is relief and rest.

20 Now when the king came to the city he inquired of his friends concerning the palace which Judas that is called Thomas was building for him. And they told him: Neither hath he built a palace nor done aught else

of that he promised to perform, but he goeth about the cities and countries, and whatsoever he hath he giveth unto the poor, and teacheth of a new God, and healeth the sick, and driveth out devils, and doeth many other wonderful things; and we think him to be a sorcerer. Yet his compassions and his cures which are done of him freely, and moreover the simplicity and kindness of him and his faith, do declare that he is a righteous man or an apostle of the new God whom he preacheth; for he fasteth continually and prayeth, and eateth bread only, with salt, and his drink is water, and he weareth but one garment alike in fair weather and in winter, and receiveth nought of any man, and that he hath he giveth unto others. And when the king heard that, he rubbed his face with his hands, and shook his head for a long space.

21 And he sent for the merchant which had brought him, and for the apostle, and said unto him: Hast thou built me the palace? And he said: Yea. And the king said: When, then, shall we go and see it? but he answered him and said: Thou canst not see it now, but when thou departest this life, then thou shalt see it. And the king was exceeding wroth, and commanded both the merchant and Judas which is called Thomas to be put in bonds and cast into prison until he should inquire and learn unto whom the king's money had been given, and so destroy both him and the merchant.

And the apostle went unto the prison rejoicing, and said to the merchant: Fear thou nothing, only believe in the God that is preached by me, and thou shalt indeed be set free from this world, but from the world to come thou shalt receive life. And the king took thought with what death he should destroy them. And when he had determined to flay them alive and burn them with fire, in the same night Gad the king's brother fell sick, and by reason of his vexation and the deceit which the king had suffered he was greatly oppressed; and sent for the king and said unto him: O king my brother, I commit unto thee mine house and my children; for I am vexed by reason of the provocation that hath befallen thee, and lo, I die; and if thou visit not with vengeance upon the head of that sorcerer, thou wilt give my soul no rest in hell. And the king said to his brother: All this night have I considered how I should put him to death and this hath seemed good to me, to flay him and burn him with fire, both him and the merchant which brought him (Syr. Then the brother of the king said to him: And if there be anything else that is worse than this, do it to him; and I give thee charge of my house and my children).

22 And as they talked together, the soul of his brother Gad departed. And

the king mourned sore for Gad, for he loved him much, and commanded that he should be buried in royal and precious apparel (Syr. sepulchre). Now after this angels took the soul of Gad the king's brother and bore it up into heaven, showing unto him the places and dwellings that were there, and inquired of him: In which place wouldest thou dwell? And when they drew near unto the building of Thomas the apostle which he had built for the king, Gad saw it and said unto the angels: I beseech you, my lords, suffer me to dwell in one of the lowest rooms of these. And they said to him: Thou canst not dwell in this building. And he said: Wherefore? And they say unto him: This is that palace which that Christian builded for thy brother. And he said: I beseech you, my lords, suffer me to go to my brother, that I may buy this palace of him, for my brother knoweth not of what sort it is, and he will sell it unto me.

23 Then the angels let the soul of Gad go. And as they were putting his grave clothes upon him, his soul entered into him and he said to them that stood about him: Call my brother unto me, that I may ask one petition of him. Straightway therefore they told the king, saying: Thy brother is revived. And the king ran forth with a great company and came unto his brother and entered in and stood by his bed as one amazed, not being able to speak to him. And his brother said: I know and am persuaded, my brother, that if any man had asked of thee the half of thy kingdom, thou wouldest have given it him for my sake; therefore I beg of thee to grant me one favour which I ask of thee, that thou wouldest sell me that which I ask of thee. And the king answered and said: And what is it which thou askest me to sell thee? And he said: Convince me by an oath that thou wilt grant it me. And the king sware unto him: One of my possessions, whatsoever thou shalt ask, I will give thee. And he saith to him: Sell me that palace which thou hast in the heavens ? And the king said: Whence should I have a palace in the heavens? And he said: Even that which that Christian built for thee which is now in the prison, whom the merchant brought unto thee, having purchased him of one Jesus: I mean that Hebrew slave whom thou desiredst to punish as having suffered deceit at his hand: whereat I was grieved and died, and am now revived.

24 Then the king considering the matter, understood it of those eternal benefits which should come to him and which concerned him, and said: That palace I cannot sell thee, but I pray to enter into it and dwell therein and to be accounted worthy of the inhabiters of it, but if thou indeed desirest to buy such a palace, lo, the man liveth and shall build thee one

better than it. And forthwith he sent and brought out of prison the apostle and the merchant that was shut up with him, saying: I entreat thee, as a man that entreateth the minister of God, that thou wouldest pray for me and beseech him whose minister thou art to forgive me and overlook that which I have done unto thee or thought to do, and that I may become a worthy inhabiter of that dwelling for the which I took no pains, but thou hast builded it for me, labouring alone, the grace of thy God working with thee, and that I also may become a servant and serve this God whom thou preachest. And his brother also fell down before the apostle and said: I entreat and supplicate thee before thy God that I may become worthy of his ministry and service, and that it may fall to me to be worthy of the things that were shown unto me by his angels.

25 And the apostle, filled with joy, said: I praise thee, O Lord Jesu, that thou hast revealed thy truth in these men; for thou only art the God of truth, and none other, and thou art he that knoweth all things that are unknown to the most; thou, Lord, art he that in all things showest compassion and sparest men. For men by reason of the error that is in them have overlooked thee but thou hast not overlooked them. And now at my supplication and request do thou receive the king and his brother and join them unto thy fold, cleansing them with thy washing and anointing them with thine oil from the error that encompasseth them: and keep them also from the wolves, bearing them into thy meadows. And give them drink out of thine immortal fountain which is neither fouled nor drieth up; for they entreat and supplicate thee and desire to become thy servants and ministers, and for this they are content even to be persecuted of thine enemies, and for thy sake to be hated of them and to be mocked and to die, like as thou for our sake didst suffer all these things, that thou mightest preserve us, thou that art Lord and verily the good shepherd. And do thou grant them to have confidence in thee alone, and the succour that cometh of thee and the hope of their salvation which they look for from thee alone; and that they may be grounded in thy mysteries and receive the perfect good of thy graces and gifts, and flourish in thy ministry and come to perfection in thy Father.

26 Being therefore wholly set upon the apostle, both the king Gundaphorus and Gad his brother followed him and departed not from him at all, and they also relieved them that had need giving unto all and refreshing all. And they besought him that they also might henceforth receive the seal of the word, saying unto him: Seeing that our souls are

at leisure and eager toward God, give thou us the seal; for we have heard thee say that the God whom thou preachest knoweth his own sheep by his seal. And the apostle said unto them: I also rejoice and entreat you to receive this seal, and to partake with me in this eucharist and blessing of the Lord, and to be made perfect therein. For this is the Lord and God of all, even Jesus Christ whom I preach, and he is the father of truth, in whom I have taught you to believe. And he commanded them to bring oil, that they might receive the seal by the oil. They brought the oil therefore, and lighted many lamps; for it was night (Syr. whom I preach: and the king gave orders that the bath should be closed for seven days, and that no man should bathe in it: and when the seven days were done, on the eighth day they three entered into the bath by night that Judas might baptize them. And many lamps were lighted in the bath).

27 And the apostle arose and sealed them. And the Lord was revealed unto them by a voice, saying: Peace be unto you brethren. And they heard his voice only, but his likeness they saw not, for they had not yet received the added sealing of the seal (Syr. had not been baptized). And the apostle took the oil and poured it upon their heads and anointed and chrismed them, and began to say (Syr. And Judas went up and stood upon the edge of the cistern and poured oil upon their heads and said):

Come, thou holy name of the Christ that is above every name.

Come, thou power of the Most High, and the compassion that is perfect.

Come, gift (charism) of the Most High.

Come, compassionate mother.

Come, communion of the male.

Come, she that revealeth the hidden mysteries.

Come, mother of the seven houses, that thy rest may be in the eighth house.

Come, elder of the five members, mind, thought, reflection, consideration, reason; communicate with these young men.

Come, holy spirit, and cleanse their veins and their heart, and give them the added seal, in the name of the Father and Son and Holy Ghost.

And when they were sealed, there appeared unto them a youth holding a lighted torch, so that their lamps became dim at the approach of the light thereof. And he went forth and was no more seen of them. And the apostle said unto the Lord: Thy light, O Lord, is not to be contained by us, and we are not able to bear it, for it is too great for our sight.

And when the dawn came and it was morning, he brake bread and made them partakers of the eucharist of the Christ. And they were glad and rejoiced.

And many others also, believing, were added to them, and came into the refuge of the Saviour.*

28 And the apostle ceased not to preach and to say unto them: Ye men and women, boys and girls, young men and maidens, strong men and aged, whether bond or free, abstain from fornication and covetousness

* Note (by Professor F. C. Burliitt, D.D.):

In the Acts of Thomas, 27, the apostle, being about to baptize Gundaphorus the king of India with his brother Gad, invokes the holy name of the Christ, and among other invocations says (according to the best Greek text):

'Come, O elder of the five members, mind, idea, thoughtfulness, consideration, reasoning, communicate with these youths.'

What is the essential distinction of these five words for 'mind', and what is meant by the 'elder' (presbuteros, Greek)? We turn to the Syriac, as the original language in which our tale was composed though our present text, which rests here on two manuscripts, has now and then been bowdlerized in the direction of more conventional phraseology, a process that the Greek has often escaped. Here in the Syriac we find (Wright, p.193, l.13; E.Tr., p.166, last line but one):

'Come, Messenger of reconciliation, and communicate with the minds of these youths.'

The word for 'Come' is fem., while 'Messenger' (Izgadda) is masc. This is because the whole prayer is an invocation of the Holy Spirit, which in old Syriac is invariably treated as feminine. The word for Messenger is that used in the Manichaean cosmogony for a heavenly Spirit sent from the Divine Light: this Spirit appeared as androgynous, so that the use of the word here with the feminine verb is not inappropriate. It further leads us to look out for other indications of Manichaean phraseology in the passage. But first it suggests to us that [presbuteros] in our passage is a corruption of, or is used for, [presbeutes], 'an ambassador'.

As for the five words for 'mind', they are clearly the equivalents of [hauna, mad'a, re'yana, mahshebhatha, tar'itha], named by Theodore bar Khoni as the Five Shekhinas, or Dwellings, or Manifestations, of the Father of Greatness, the title by which the Manichaeans spoke of the ultimate Source of Light. There is a good discussion of these five words by M. A. Kugener in F. Cumont's [Recherches sur le Manicheisme] i, p. 10, note 3. In English we may say:

hauna means 'sanity', mad'a means 'reason', re'yana means 'mind', mahshabhetha means 'imagination', tar'itha means 'intention'

The Greek terms, used here and also in Acta Archelai, are in my opinion merely equivalents for the Syriac terms.

and the service of the belly: for under these three heads all iniquity cometh about. For fornication blindeth the mind and darkeneth the eyes of the soul, and is an impediment to the life (conversation) of the body, turning the whole man unto weakness and casting the whole body into sickness. And greed putteth the soul into fear and shame; being within the body it seizeth upon the goods of others, and is under fear lest if it restore other men's goods to their owner it be put to shame. And the service of the belly casteth the soul into thoughts and cares and vexations, taking thought lest it come to be in want, and have need of those things that are far from it. If, then, ye be rid of these ye become free of care and grief and fear, and that abideth with you which was said by the Saviour: Take no thought for the morrow, for the morrow shall take thought for the things of itself. Remember also that word of him of whom I spake: Look at the ravens and see the fowls of the heaven, that they neither sow nor reap nor gather into barns, and God dispenseth unto them; how much more unto you, O ye of little faith? But look ye for his coming and have your hope in him and believe on his name. For he is the judge of quick and dead, and he giveth to every one according to their deeds, and at his coming and his latter appearing no man hath any word of excuse when he is to be judged by him, as though he had not heard. For his heralds do proclaim in the four quarters (climates) of the world. Repent ye, therefore, and believe the promise and receive the yoke of meekness and the light burden, that ye may live and not die. These things get, these keep. Come forth of the darkness that the light may receive you! Come unto him that is indeed good, that ye may receive grace of him and implant his sign in your souls. 29 And when he had thus spoken, some of them that stood by said: It is time for the creditor to receive the debt. And he said unto them: He that is lord of the debt desireth always to receive more; but let us give him that which is due. And he blessed them, and took bread and oil and herbs and salt and blessed and gave unto them; but he himself continued his fast, for the Lord's day was coming on (Syr. And he himself ate, because the Sunday was dawning).

And when night fell and he slept, the Lord came and stood at his head, saying: Thomas, rise early, and having blessed them all, after the prayer and the ministry go by the eastern road two miles and there will I show thee my glory: for by thy going shall many take refuge with me, and thou shalt bring to light the nature and power of the enemy. And he rose up from sleep and said unto the brethren that were with him: Children, the Lord would accomplish somewhat by me to-day, but let us pray, and entreat of him that we may have no impediment toward him, but that as at all times, so now also it may be done according to his desire and will by us. And having so said, he laid his hands on them and blessed them, and brake the bread of the eucharist and gave it them, saying: This Eucharist shall be unto you for compassion and mercy, and not unto judgement and retribution. And they said Amen.

THE THIRD ACT

Concerning the servant

30 And the apostle went forth to go where the Lord had bidden him; and when he was near to the second mile (stone) and had turned a little out of the way, he saw the body of a comely youth lying, and said: Lord, is it for this that thou hast brought me forth, to come hither that I might see this (trial) temptation? thy will therefore be done as thou desirest. And he began to pray and to say: O Lord, the judge of quick and dead, of the quick that stand by and the dead that lie here, and master and father of all things; and father not only of the souls that are in bodies but of them that have gone forth of them, for of the souls also that are in pollutions (al. bodies) thou art lord and judge; come thou at this hour wherein I call upon thee and show forth thy glory upon him that lieth here. And he turned himself unto them that followed him and said: This thing is not come to pass without cause, but the enemy hath effected it and brought it about that he may assault (?) us thereby; and see ye that he hath not made use of another sort, nor wrought through any other creature save that which is his subject.

31 And when he had so said, a great (Syr. black) serpent (dragon) came out of a hole, beating with his head and shaking his tail upon the ground, and with (using) a loud voice said unto the apostle: I will tell before thee the cause wherefore I slew this man, since thou art come hither for that

end, to reprove my works. And the apostle said: Yea, say on. And the serpent: There is a certain beautiful woman in this village over against us; and as she passed by me (or my place) I saw her and was enamoured of her, and I followed her and kept watch upon her; and I found this youth kissing her, and he had intercourse with her and did other shameful acts with her: and for me it was easy to declare them before thee, for I know that thou art the twin brother of the Christ and always abolishest our nature (Syr. easy for me to say, but to thee I do not dare to utter them because I know that the ocean-flood of the Messiah will destroy our nature): but because I would not affright her, I slew him not at that time, but waited for him till he passed by in the evening and smote and slew him, and especially because he adventured to do this upon the Lord's day.

And the apostle inquired of him, saying: Tell me of what seed and of what race thou art.

32 And he said unto him: I am a reptile of the reptile nature and noxious son of the noxious father: of him that hurt and smote the four brethren which stood upright (om. Syr.: the elements or four cardinal points may be meant) I am son to him that sitteth on a throne over all the earth that receiveth back his own from them that borrow: I am son to him that girdeth about the sphere: and I am kin to him that is outside the ocean, whose tail is set in his own mouth: I am he that entered through the barrier (fence) into paradise and spake with Eve the things which my father bade me speak unto her: I am he that kindled and inflamed Cain to kill his own brother, and on mine account did thorns and thistles grow up in the earth: I am he that cast down the angels from above and bound them in lusts after women, that children born of earth might come of them and I might work my will in them: I am he that hardened Pharaoh's heart that he should slay the children of Israel and enslave them with the yoke of cruelty: I am he that caused the multitude to err in the wilderness when they made the calf: I am he that inflamed Herod and enkindled Caiaphas unto false accusation of a lie before Pilate; for this was fitting to me: I am he that stirred up Judas and bribed him to deliver up the Christ: I am he that inhabiteth and holdeth the deep of hell (Tartarus), but the Son of God hath wronged me, against my will, and taken (chosen) them that were his own from me: I am kin to him that is to come from the east, unto whom also power is given to do what he will upon the earth.

33 And when that serpent had spoken these things in the hearing of all the people, the apostle lifted up his voice on high and said: Cease

thou henceforth, O most shameless one, and be put to confusion and die wholly, for the end of thy destruction is come, and dare not to tell of what thou hast done by them that have become subject unto thee. And I charge thee in the name of that Jesus who until now contendeth with you for the men that are his own, that thou suck out thy venom which thou hast put into this man, and draw it forth and take it from him. But the serpent said: Not yet is the end of our time come as thou hast said. Wherefore compellest thou me to take back that which I have put into this man, and to die before my time? for mine own father, when he shall draw forth and suck out that which he hath cast into the creation, then shall his end come. And the apostle said unto him: Show, then, now the nature of thy father. And the serpent came near and set his mouth upon the wound of the young man and sucked forth the gall out of it. And by little and little the colour of the young man which was as purple, became white, but the serpent swelled up. And when the serpent had drawn up all the gall into himself, the young man leapt up and stood, and ran and fell at the apostle's feet: but the serpent being swelled up, burst and died, and his venom and gall were shed forth; and in the place where his venom was shed there came a great gulf, and that serpent was swallowed up therein. And the apostle said unto the king and his brother: Take workmen and fill up that place, and lay foundations and build houses upon them, that it may be a dwelling-place for strangers.

34 But the youth said unto the apostle with many tears: Wherein have I sinned against thee? for thou art a man that hast two forms, and wheresoever thou wilt, there thou art found, and art restrained of no man, as I behold. For I saw that man that stood by thee and said unto thee: I have many wonders to show forth by thy means and I have great works to accomplish by thee, for which thou shalt receive a reward; and thou shalt make many to live, and they shall be in rest in light eternal as children of God. Do thou then, saith he, speaking unto thee of me, quicken this youth that hath been stricken of the enemy and be at all times his overseer. Well, therefore, art thou come hither, and well shalt thou depart again unto him, and yet he never shall leave thee at any time. But I am become without care or reproach: and he hath enlightened me from the care of the night and I am at rest from the toil of the day: and I am set free from him that provoked me to do thus, sinning against him that taught me to do contrary thereto: and I have lost him that is the kinsman of the night that compelled me to sin by his own deeds, and have found him that is of the light, and is

my kinsman. I have lost him that darkeneth and blindeth his own subjects that they may not know what they do and, being ashamed at their own works, may depart from him, and their works come to an end; and have found him whose works are light and his deeds truth, which if a man doeth he repenteth not of them. And I have left him with whom lying abideth, and before whom darkness goeth as a veil, and behind him followeth shame, shameless in indolence; and I have found him that showeth me fair things that I may take hold on them, even the son of the truth that is akin unto concord, who scattereth away the mist and enlighteneth his own creation, and healeth the wounds thereof and overthroweth the enemies thereof. But I beseech thee, O man of God, cause me to behold him again, and to see him that is now become hidden from me, that I may also hear his voice whereof I am not able to express the wonder, for it belongeth not to the nature of this bodily organ.

[Before this speech Syr. (Wright) inserts one of equal length, chiefly about man's free will and fall. But the fifth-century palimpsest edited by Mrs. Lewis agrees with the Greek.]

35 And the apostle answered him, saying: If thou depart from these things whereof thou hast received knowledge, as thou hast said, and if thou know who it is that hath wrought this in thee, and learn and become a hearer of him whom now in thy fervent love thou seekest; thou shalt both see him and be with him for ever, and in his rest shalt thou rest, and shalt be in his joy. But if thou be slackly disposed toward him and turn again unto thy former deeds, and leave that beauty and that bright countenance which now was showed thee, and forget the shining of his light which now thou desirest, not only wilt thou be bereaved of this life but also of that which is to come and thou wilt depart unto him whom thou saidst thou hadst lost, and will no more behold him whom thou saidst thou hadst found.

36 And when the apostle had said this, he went into the city holding the hand of that youth, and saying unto him: These things which thou hast seen, my child, are but a few of the many which God hath, for he doth not give us good tidings concerning these things that are seen, but greater things than these doth he promise us; but so long as we are in the body we are not able to speak and show forth those which he shall give unto our souls. If we say that he giveth us light, it is this which is seen, and we have it: and if we say it of wealth, which is and appeareth in the world, we name it (we speak of something which is in the world, Syr.), and we

need it not, for it hath been said: Hardly shall a rich man enter into the kingdom of heaven: and if we speak of apparel of raiment wherewith they that are luxurious in this life are clad, it is named (we mention something that nobles wear, Syr.), and it hath been said: They that wear soft raiment are in the houses of kings. And if of costly banquets, concerning these we have received a commandment to beware of them, not to be weighed down With reveling and drunkenness and cares of this life -speaking of things that are- and it hath been said: Take no thought for your life (soul), what ye shall eat or what ye shall drink, neither for your body, what ye shall put on, for the soul is more than the meat and the body than the raiment. And of rest, if we speak of this temporal rest, a judgement is appointed for this also. But we speak of the world which is above, of God and angels, of watchers and holy ones of the immortal (ambrosial) food and the drink of the true vine, of raiment that endureth and groweth not old, of things which eye hath not seen nor ear heard, neither have they entered into the heart of sinful men, the things which God hath prepared for them that love him. Of these things do we converse and of these do we bring good tidings. Do thou therefore also believe on him that thou mayest live, and put thy trust in him, and thou shalt not die. For he is not persuaded with gifts, that thou shouldest offer them to him, neither is he in need of sacrifices, that thou shouldest sacrifice unto him. But look thou unto him, and he will not overlook thee; and turn unto him, and he will not forsake thee. For his comeliness and his beauty will make thee wholly desirous to love him: and indeed he permitteth thee not to turn thyself away.

37 And when the apostle had said these things unto that youth, a great multitude joined themselves unto them. And the apostle looked and saw them raising themselves on high that they might see him, and they were going up into high places; and the apostle said unto them: Ye men that are come unto the assembly of Christ, and would believe on Jesus, take example hereby, and see that if ye be not lifted up, ye cannot see me who am little, and are not able to spy me out who am like unto you. If, then, ye cannot see me who am like you unless ye lift yourselves up a little from the earth, how can ye see him that dwelleth in the height and now is found in the depth, unless ye first lift yourselves up out of your former conversation, and your unprofitable deeds, and your desires that abide not, and the wealth that is left here, and the possession of earth that groweth old, and the raiment that corrupteth, and the beauty that waxeth old and

vanisheth away, and yet more out of the whole body wherein all these things are stored up, and which groweth old and becometh dust, returning unto its own nature? For it is the body which maintaineth all these things. But rather believe on our Lord Jesus Christ, vvhom we preach, that your hope may be in him and in him ye may have life world without end, that he may become your fellow traveller in this land of error, and may be to you an harbour in this troublous sea. And he shall be to you a fountain springing up in this thirsty land and a chamber fill of food in this place of them that hunger, and a rest unto your souls, yea, and a physician for your bodies.

38 Then the multitude of them that were gathered together hearing these things wept, and said unto the apostle: O man of God, the God whom thou preachest, we dare not say that we are his, for the works which we have done are alien unto him and not pleasing to him; but if he will have compassion on us and pity us and save us, overlooking our former deeds, and will set us free from the evils which we committed being in error, and not impute them unto us nor make remembrance of our former sins, we will become his servants and will accomplish his will unto the end. And the apostle answered them and said: He reckoneth not against you, neither taketh account of the sins which ye committed being in error, but overlooketh your transgressions which ye have done in ignorance.

THE FOURTH ACT

Concerning the colt

39 And while the apostle yet stood in the highway and spake with the multitude, A she ass's colt came and stood before him (Syr. adds, And Judas said: It is not without the direction of God that this colt has come hither. But to thee I say, O colt that by the grace of our Lord there shall be given to thee speech before these multitudes who are standing here; and do thou say whatsoever thou wilt, that they may believe in the God of truth whom we preach. And the mouth of the colt was opened, and it spake by the power of our Lord and said to him) and opened its mouth and said: Thou twin of Christ, apostle of the Most High and initiate in

the hidden word of Christ who receivest his secret oracles, fellow worker with the Son of God, who being free hast become a bondman, and being sold hast brought many into liberty. Thou kinsman of the great race that hath condemned the enemy and redeemed his own, that hast become an occasion of life unto man in the land of the Indians; for thou hast come (against thy will, Syr.) unto men that were in error, and by thy appearing and thy divine words they are now turning unto the God of truth which sent thee: mount and sit upon me and repose thyself until thou enter into the city. And the apostle answered and said: O Jesu Christ (Son) that understandest the perfect mercy! O tranquillity and quiet that now art spoken of (speakest, Syr.) by (among) brute beasts! O hidden rest, that art manifested by thy working, Saviour of us and nourisher, keeping us and resting in alien bodies! O Saviour of our souls! spring that is sweet and unfailing; fountain secure and clear and never polluted; defender and helper in the fight of thine own servants, turning away and scaring the enemy from us, that fightest in many battles for us and makest us conquerors in all; our true and undefeated champion (athlete); our holy and victorious captain: glorious and giving unto thine own a joy that never passeth away, and a relief wherein is none affliction; good shepherd that givest thyself for thine own sheep, and hast vanquished the wolf and redeemed thine own lambs and led them into a good pasture: we glorify and praise thee and thine invisible Father and thine holy spirit [and] the mother of all creation.

40 And when the apostle had said these things, all the multitude that were there looked upon him, expecting to hear what he would answer to the colt. And the apostle stood a long time as it were astonied, and looked up into heaven and said to the colt: Of whom art thou and to whom belongest thou? for marvelous are the things that are shown forth by thy mouth, and amazing and such as are hidden from the many. And the colt answered and said: I am of that stock that served Balaam, and thy lord also and teacher sat upon one that appertained unto me by race. And I also have now been sent to give thee rest by thy sitting upon me: and (that) I may receive (Syr. these may be confirmed in) faith, and unto me may be added that portion which now I shall receive by thy service wherewith I serve thee; and when I have ministered unto thee, it shall be taken from me. And the apostle said unto him: He is able who granted thee this gift, to cause it to be fulfilled unto the end in thee and in them that belong unto thee by race: for as to this mystery I am weak and powerless. And he would

not sit upon him. But the colt besought and entreated him that he might be blessed of him by ministering unto him. Then the apostle mounted him and sat upon him; and they followed him, some going before and some following after, and all of them ran, desiring to see the end, and how he would dismiss the colt.

41 But when he came near to the city gates he dismounted from him, saying: Depart, and be thou kept safe where thou wert. And straightway the colt fell to the ground at the apostle's feet and died. And all they that were present were sorry and said to the apostle: Bring him to life and raise him up. But he answered and said unto them: I indeed am able to raise him by the name of Jesus Christ: but this is by all means expedient (or, this is [NOT] by any means expedient). For he that gave him speech that he might talk was able to cause that he should not die; and I raise him not, not as being unable, but because this is that which is expedient and profitable for him. And he bade them that were present to dig a trench and bury his body and they did as they were commanded.

THE FIFTH ACT

Concerning the devil that took up his abode in the woman

42 And the apostle entered into the city and all the multitude followed him. And he thought to go unto the parents of the young man whom he had made alive when he was slain by the serpent: for they earnestly besought him to come unto them and enter into their house. But a very beautiful woman on a sudden uttered an exceeding loud cry, saying: O Apostle of the new God that art come into India, and servant of that holy and only good God; for by thee is he preached, the Saviour of the souls that come unto him, and by thee are healed the bodies of them that are tormented by the enemy, and thou art he that is become an occasion of life unto all that turn unto him: command me to be brought before thee that I may tell thee what hath befallen me, and peradventure of thee I may have hope, and these that stand by thee may be more confident in the God whom thou preachest. For I am not a little tormented by the adversary now this five years' space [one Greek MS. And the apostle bade her come unto him, and

the woman stood before him and said: I, O servant of him that is indeed God am a woman: the rest have, As a woman] I was sitting at the first in quiet, and peace encompassed me on every side and I had no care for anything, for I took no thought for any other.

43 And it fell out one day that as I came out from the bath there met me a man troubled and disturbed, and his voice and speech seemed to me exceeding faint and dim; and he stood before me and said: I and thou will be in one love and we will have intercourse together as a man with his wife; And I answered and said to him: I never had to do with my betrothed, for I refused to marry, and how shall I yield myself to thee that wouldest have intercourse with me in adulterous wise? And having so said, I passed on, and I said to my handmaid that was with me: Sawest thou that youth and his shamelessness, how boldly he spake with me, and had no shame? but she said to me: I saw an old man speaking to thee. And when I was in mine house and had dined my soul suggested unto me some suspicion and especially because he was seen of me in two forms; and having this in my mind I fell asleep. He came, therefore, in that night and was joined unto me in his foul intercourse. And when it was day I saw him and fled from him, and on the night following that he came and abused me; and now as thou seest me I have spent five years being troubled by him, and he hath not departed from me. But I know and am persuaded that both devils and spirits and destroyers are subject unto thee and are filled with trembling at thy prayers: pray thou therefore for me and drive away from me the devil that ever troubleth me, that I also may be set free and be gathered unto the nature that is mine from the beginning, and receive the grace that hath been given unto my kindred.

44 And the apostle said: O evil that cannot be restrained! O shamelessness of the enemy! O envious one that art never at rest! O hideous one that subduest the comely! O thou of many forms! As he will he appeareth, but his essence cannot be changed. O the crafty and faithless one! O the bitter tree whose fruits are like unto him! O the devil that overcometh them that are alien to him! O the deceit that useth impudence! O the wickedness that creepeth like a serpent, and that is of his kindred! (Syr. wrongly adds a clause bidding the devil show himself.) And when the apostle said this, the malicious one came and stood before him, no man seeing him save the woman and the apostle, and with an exceeding loud voice said in the hearing of all:

45 What have we to do with thee, thou apostle of the Most High! What

have we to do with thee, thou servant of Jesus Christ? What have we to do with thee, thou counsellor of the holy Son of God? Wherefore wilt thou destroy us, whereas our time is not yet come? Wherefore wilt thou take away our power? for unto this hour we had hope and time remaining to us. What have we to do with thee? Thou hast power over thine own, and we over ours. Wherefore wilt thou act tyrannously against us, when thou thyself teachest others not to act tyrannously? Wherefore dost thou crave other men's goods and not suffice thyself with thine own? Wherefore art thou made like unto the Son of God which hath done us wrong? for thou resemblest him altogether as if thou wert born of him. For we thought to have brought him under the yoke like as we have the rest, but he turned and made us subject unto him: for we knew him not; but he deceived us with his form of all uncomeliness and his poverty and his neediness: for seeing him to be such, we thought that he was a man wearing flesh, and knew not that it is he that giveth life unto men. And he gave us power over our own, and that we should not in this present time leave them but have our walk in them: but thou wouldest get more than thy due and that which was given thee, and afflict us altogether.

46 And having said this the devil wept, saying: I leave thee, my fairest consort, whom long since I found and rested in thee; I forsake thee, my sure sister, my beloved in whom I was well pleased. What I shall do I know not, or on whom I shall call that he may hear me and help me. I know what I will do: I will depart unto some place where the report of this man hath not been heard, and peradventure I shall call thee, my beloved by another name (Syr. for thee my beloved I shall find a substitute). And he lifted up his voice and said: Abide in peace for thou hast taken refuge with one greater than I, but I will depart and seek for one like thee, and if I find her not, I will return unto thee again: for I know that whilst thou art near unto this man thou hast a refuge in him, but when he departeth thou wilt be such as thou wast before he appeared, and him thou wilt forget, and I shall have opportunity and confidence: but now I fear the name of him that hath saved thee. And having so said the devil vanished out of sight: only when he departed fire and smoke were seen there: and all that stood there were astonied.

47 And the apostle seeing it, said unto them: This devil hath shown nought that is alien or strange to him, but his own nature, wherein also he shall be consumed, for verily the fire shall destroy him utterly and the smoke of it shall be scattered abroad. And he began to say:

Jesu, the hidden mystery that hath been revealed unto us, thou art he that hast shown unto us many mysteries; thou that didst call me apart from all my fellows and spakest unto me three (one, Syr.) words wherewith I am inflamed, and am not able to speak them unto others. Jesu, man that wast slain, dead buried! Jesu, God of God, Saviour that quickenest the dead, and healest the sick! Jesu, that wert in need like [a man poor] and savest as one that hath no need, that didst catch the fish for the breakfast and the dinner and madest all satisfied with a little bread. Jesu, that didst rest from the weariness of wayfaring like a man, and walkedst on the waves like a God.

48 Jesu most high, voice arising from perfect mercy, Saviour of all, the right hand of the light, overthrowing the evil one in his own nature, and gathering all his nature into one place; thou of many forms, that art only begotten, first-born of many brethren God of the Most High God, man despised until now (Syr. and humble). Jesu Christ that neglectest us not when we call upon thee, that art become an occasion of life unto all mankind, that for us wast judged and shut up in prison, and loosest all that are in bonds, that wast called a deceiver and redeemest thine own from error: I beseech thee for these that stand here and believe on thee, for they entreat to obtain thy gifts, having good hope in thy help, and having their refuge in thy greatness; they hold their hearing ready to listen unto the words that are spoken by us. Let thy peace come and tabernacle in them and renew them from their former deeds, and let them put off the old man with his deeds, and put on the new that now is proclaimed unto them by me.

49 And he laid his hands on them and blessed them, saying: The grace of our Lord Jesus Christ shall be upon you for ever. And they said, Amen. And the woman besought him, saying: O apostle of the Most High, give me the seal, that that enemy return not again unto me. Then he caused her to come near unto him (Syr. went to a river which was close by there), and laid his hands upon her and sealed her in the name of the Father and the Son and the Holy Ghost; and many others also were sealed with her. And the apostle bade his minister (deacon) to set forth a table; and he set forth a stool which they found there, and spread a linen cloth upon it and set on the bread of blessing; and the apostle stood by it and said: Jesu, that hast accounted us worthy to partake of the eucharist of thine holy body and blood, lo, we are bold to draw near unto thine eucharist and to call upon thine holy name: come thou and communicate unto us (Syr. adds more).

50 And he began to say: Come, O perfect compassion, Come O communion of the male, Come, she that knoweth the mysteries of him that is chosen, Come, she that hath part in all the combats of the noble champion (athlete), Come, the silence that revealeth the great things of the whole greatness, Come, she that manifesteth the hidden things and maketh the unspeakable things plain, the holy dove that beareth the twin young, Come, the hidden mother, Come, she that is manifest in her deeds and giveth joy and rest unto them that are joined unto her: Come and communicate with us in this eucharist which we celebrate in thy name and in the love-feast wherein we are gathered together at thy calling. (Syr. has other clauses and not few variants.) And having so said he marked out the cross upon the bread, and brake it, and began to distribute it. And first he gave unto the woman, saying: This shall be unto thee for remission of sins and eternal transgressions (Syr. and for the everlasting resurrection). And after her he gave unto all the others also which had received the seal (Syr. and said to them: Let this eucharist be unto you for life and rest, and not for judgement and vengeance. And they said, Amen. Cf. 29 fin.).

THE SIXTH ACT

Of the youth that murdered the Woman.

51 Now there was a certain youth who had wrought an abominable deed, and he came near and received of the eucharist with his mouth: but his two hands withered up, so that he could no more put them unto his own mouth. And they that were there saw him and told the apostle what had befallen; and the apostle called him and said unto him: Tell me, my child, and be not ashamed, what was it that thou didst and camest hither? for the eucharist of the Lord hath convicted thee. For this gift which passeth among many doth rather heal them that with faith and love draw near thereto, but thee it hath withered away; and that which is come to pass hath not befallen without some effectual cause. And the Youth, being convicted by the eucharist of the Lord, came and tell at the apostle's feet and besought him, saying: I have done an evil deed, yet I thought to do somewhat good. I was enamoured of a woman that dwelleth at an

inn without the city, and she also loved me; and when I heard of thee and believed, that thou proclaimest a living God, I came and received of thee the seal with the rest; for thou saidst: Whosoever shall partake in the polluted union, and especially in adultery, he shall not have life with the God whom I preach. Whereas therefore I loved her much, I entreated her and would have persuaded her to become my consort in chastity and pure conversation, which thou also teachest: but she would not. When, therefore, she consented not, I took a sword and slew her: for I could not endure to see her commit adultery with another man.

52 When the apostle heard this he said: O insane union how ruinest thou unto shamelessness! O unrestrained lust, how hast thou stirred up this man to do this! O work of the serpent, how art thou enraged against thine own! And the apostle bade water to be brought to him in a basin; and when the water was brought, he said: Come, ye waters from the living waters, that were sent unto us, the true from the true, the rest that was sent unto us from the rest, the power of salvation that cometh from that power which conquereth all things and subdueth them unto its own will: come and dwell in these waters, that the gift of the Holy Ghost may be perfectly consummated in them. And he said unto the youth: Go, wash thy hands in these waters. And when he had washed they were restored; and the apostle said unto him: Believest thou in our Lord Jesus Christ that he is able to do all things? And he said: Though I be the least, yet I believe. But I committed this deed thinking that I was doing somewhat good: for I besought her as I told thee, but she would not obey me, to keep herself chaste.

53 And the apostle said to him: Come, let us go unto the inn where thou didst commit this deed. And the youth went before the apostle in the way, and when they came to the inn they found her Lying dead. And the apostle when he saw her was sorry, for she was a comely girl. And he commanded her to be brought into the midst of the inn: and they laid her on a bed and brought her forth and set her down in the midst of the court of the inn. And the apostle laid his hand upon her and began to say: Jesu, who always showest thyself unto us; for this is thy will, that we should at all times seek thee, and thyself hast given us this power, to ask and to receive, and hast not only permitted this, but hast taught us to pray: who art not seen of our bodily eyes, but art never hidden from the eyes of our soul, and in thine aspect art concealed, but in thy works art manifested unto us: and in thy many acts we have known thee so far as we are able, and thyself

hast given us thy gifts without measure, saying: Ask and it shall be given unto you, seek and ye shall find, knock and it shall be opened unto you: we beseech thee, therefore, having the fear (suspicion) of our sins; and we ask of thee, not riches, not gold, not silver, not possessions, not aught else of the things which come of the earth and return again unto the earth; but this we ask of thee and entreat, that in thine holy name thou wouldest raise up the woman that lieth here, by thy power, to the glory and faith of them that stand by.

54 And he said unto the youth (Syr. ' Stretch thy mind towards our Lord,' and he signed him with the cross), having signed (sealed) him: Go and take hold on her hand and say unto her: I with my hands slew thee with iron, and with my hands in the faith of Jesus I raise thee up. So the youth went to her and stood by her, saying: I have believed in thee, Christ Jesu. And he looked unto Judas Thomas the apostle and said to him: Pray for me that my Lord may come to my help, whom I also call upon. And he laid his hand upon her hand and said: Come, Lord Jesu Christ: unto her grant thou life and unto me the earnest of faith in thee. And straightway as he drew her hand she sprang up and sat up, looking upon the great company that stood by. And she saw the apostle also standing over against her, and leaving the bed she leapt forth and fell at his feet and caught hold on his raiment, saying: I beseech thee, my lord where is that other that was with thee, who left me not to remain in that fearful and cruel place, but delivered me unto thee, saying: Take thou this woman, that she may be made perfect, and hereafter be gathered into her place?

55 And the apostle said unto her: Relate unto us where thou hast been. And she answered: Dost thou who wast with me and unto whom I was delivered desire to hear? And she began to say: [This description of hell-torments is largely derived from the Apocalypse of Peter] A man took me who was hateful to look upon altogether black, and his raiment exceedingly foul, and took me away to a place wherein were many pits (chasms), and a great stench and hateful odour issued thence. And he caused me to look into every pit, and I saw in the (first) pit flaming fire, and wheels of fire ran round there, and souls were hanged upon those wheels, and were dashed (broken) against each other; and very great crying and howling was there, and there was none to deliver. And that man said to me: These souls are of thy tribe, and when the number of their days is accomplished (lit. in the days of the number) they are (were) delivered unto torment and affliction, and then are others brought in in their stead, and likewise these

60

into another place. These are they that have reversed the intercourse of male and female. And I looked and saw infants heaped one upon another and struggling with each other as they lay on them. And he answered and said to me: These are the children of those others, and therefore are they set here for a testimony against them. (Syr. omits this clause of the children, and lengthens and dilutes the preceding speech.)

56 And he took me unto another pit, and I stooped and looked and saw mire and worms welling up, and souls wallowing there, and a great gnashing of teeth was heard thence from them. And that man said unto me: These are the souls of women which forsook their husbands and committed adultery with others, and are brought into this torment. Another pit he showed me whereinto I stooped and looked and saw souls hanging, some by the tongue, some by the hair, some by the hands, and some head downward by the feet, and tormented (smoked) with smoke and brimstone; concerning whom that man that was with me answered me: The souls which are hanged by the tongue are slanderers, that uttered Lying and shameful words, and were not ashamed, and they that are hanged by the hair are unblushing ones which had no modesty and went about in the world bareheaded; and they that are hanged by the hands, these are they that took away and stole other men's goods, and never gave aught to the needy nor helped the afflicted, but did so, desiring to take all, and had no thought at all of justice or of the law; and they that hang upside down by the feet, these are they that lightly and readily ran in evil ways and disorderly paths, not visiting the sick nor escorting them that depart this life, and therefore each and every soul receiveth that which was done by it. (Syr. omits almost the whole section.)

57 Again he took me and showed me a cave exceeding dark, breathing out a great stench, and many souls were looking out desiring to get somewhat of the air, but their keepers suffered them not to look forth. And he that was with me said: This is the prison of those souls which thou sawest: for when they have fulfilled their torments for that which each did, thereafter do others succeed them: and there be some that are wholly consumed and (some, Syr.) that are delivered over unto other torments. And they that kept the souls which were in the dark cave said unto the man that had taken me: Give her unto us that we may bring her in unto the rest until the time cometh for her to be delivered unto torment. But he answered them: I give her not unto you, for I fear him that delivered her to me: for I was not charged to leave her here, but I take her back with

me until I shall receive order concerning her. And he took me and brought me unto another place wherein were men being sharply tormented (Syr. where men were). And he that was like unto thee took me and delivered me to thee, saying thus to thee: Take her, for she is one of the sheep that have gone astray. And I was taken by thee, and now am I before thee. I beseech thee, therefore, and supplicate that I may not depart unto those places of punishment which I have seen.

58 And the apostle said: Ye have heard what this woman hath related: and there are not these torments only, but others also, worse than these; and ye, if ye turn not unto this God whom I preach, and abstain from your former works and the deeds which ye committed without knowledge, shall have your end in those torments. Believe therefore on Christ Jesus, and he will forgive you the sins ye have committed hitherto, and will cleanse you from all your bodily lusts that abide on the earth, and will heal you of all your trespasses which follow you and depart with you and are found upon (before) you. Put off therefore every one of you the old man, and put on the new, and forsake your former walk and conversation; and let them that stole steal no more, but live by labouring and working; and let the adulterous no more fornicate, lest they deliver themselves unto eternal torment; for adultery is before God exceeding evil beyond other sins. And put away from you covetousness and Lying and drunkenness and slandering, and render not evil for evil: for all these things are strange and alien unto the God who is preached by me: but rather walk ye in faith and meekness and holiness and hope, wherein God delighteth, that ye may become his own, expecting of him the gifts which some few only do receive.

59 All the people therefore believed and gave their souls obediently unto the living God and Christ Jesus, rejoicing in the blessed works of the Most High and in his holy service. And they brought much money for the service of the widows: for the apostle had them gathered together in the cities, and unto all of them he sent provision by his own ministers (deacons), both clothes and nourishment. And he himself ceased not preaching and speaking to them and showing that this is Jesus Christ whom the scriptures proclaimed, who is come and was crucified, and raised the third day from the dead. And next he showed them plainly, beginning from the prophets, the things concerning the Christ, that it was necessary that he should come, and that in him should be accomplished all things that were foretold of him. And the fame of him went forth into all

the cities and countries, and all that had sick or them that were oppressed by unclean spirits brought them, and some they laid in the way whereby he should pass, and he healed them all by the power of the Lord. Then all that were healed by him said with one accord: Glory be to thee, Jesu, who hast granted us all alike healing through thy servant and apostle Thomas. And now being whole and rejoicing, we beseech thee that we may be of thy flock, and be numbered among thy sheep; receive us therefore, Lord, and impute not unto us our transgressions and our former faults which we committed being in ignorance.

60 And the apostle said: Glory be to the only-begotten of the Father! Glory be to the first-born of many brethren! Glory be to thee, the defender and helper of them that come unto thy refuge! that sleepest not, and awakest them that are asleep that livest and givest life to them that lie in death! O God Jesu Christ, Son of the living God, redeemer and helper, refuge and rest of all that are weary (labour) in thy work, giver of healing to them that for thy name s sake bear the burden and heat of the day: we give thanks for (to) the gifts that are given us of thee and granted us by thy help and thy dispensation that cometh unto us from thee.

61 Perfect thou therefore these things in us unto the end that we may have the boldness that is in thee: look upon us for for thy sake have we forsaken our homes and our parents, and for thy sake have we gladly and willingly become strangers: look upon us, Lord, for we have forsaken our own possessions for thy sake, that we might gain thee the possession that cannot be taken away: look upon us, Lord, for we have forsaken them that belong unto us by race, that we might be joined unto thy kinship: look upon us, Lord, that have forsaken our fathers and mothers and fosters, that we might behold thy Father, and be satisfied with his divine food: look upon us, Lord, for for thy sake have we forsaken our bodily consorts and our earthly fruits, that we might be partakers in that enduring and true fellowship, and bring forth true fruits, whose nature is from above, which no man can take from us, with whom we shall abide and who shall abide with us.

THE SEVENTH ACT

Of the Captain

62 Now while the apostle Thomas was proclaiming throughout all India the word of God, a certain captain of the king Misdaeus (Mazdai, Syr.) came to him and said unto him: I have heard of thee that thou takest no reward of any man, but even that thou hast thou givest to them that need. For if thou didst receive rewards, I would have sent thee a great sum, and would not have come myself, for the king doeth nought without me: for I have much substance and am rich, even one of the rich men of India. And I have never done wrong to any; but the contrary hath befallen me. I have a wife, and of her I had a daughter and I am well affectioned toward her, as also nature requireth and have never made trial of another wife. Now it chanced that there was a wedding in our city, and they that made the marriage feast were well beloved of me: they came in therefore and bade me to it, bidding also my wife and her daughter. Forasmuch then as they were my good friends I could not refuse: I sent her therefore, though she desired not to go, and with them I sent also many servants: so they departed, both she and her daughter, decked with many ornaments.

63 And when it was evening and the time was come to depart from the wedding I sent lamps and torches to meet them: and I stood in the street to espy when she should come and I should see her with my daughter. And as I stood I heard a sound of lamentation. Woe for her! was heard out of every mouth. And my servants with their clothes rent came to me and told me what was done. We saw, said they, a man and a boy with him. And the man laid his hand upon thy wife, and the boy upon thy daughter: and they fled from them: and we smote (wounded) them with our swords, but our swords fell to the ground. And the same hour the women fell down, gnashing their teeth and beating their heads upon the earth and seeing this we came to tell it thee. And when I heard this of my servants I rent my clothes and smote my face with my hands, and becoming like one mad I ran along the street, and came and found them cast in the market-place; and I took them and brought them to my house, and after a long space they awaked and stood up, and sat down.

64 I began therefore to inquire of my wife: What is it that hath befallen thee? And she said to me: Knowest thou not what thou hast done unto me? for I prayed thee that I might not go to the wedding, because I was

not of even health in my body; and as I went on the way and came near to the aqueduct wherein the water floweth, I saw a black man standing over against me nodding at me with his head, and a boy like unto him standing by him; and I said to my daughter: Look at those two hideous men, whose teeth are like milk and their lips like soot. And we left them and went towards the aqueduct; and when it was sunset and we departed from the wedding, as we passed by with the young men and drew near the aqueduct, my daughter saw them first, and was affrighted and fled towards me; and after her I also beheld them coming against us: and the servants that were with us fled from them (Syr.) and they struck us, and cast down both me and my daughter. And when she had told me these things, the devils came upon them again and threw them down: and from that hour they are not able to come forth, but are shut up in one room or a second (Syr. in a room within another): and on their account I suffer much, and am distressed: for the devils throw them down wheresoever they find them, and strip them naked. I beseech and supplicate thee before God, help me and have pity on me, for it is now three years that a table hath not been set in my house, and my wife and my daughter have not sat at a table: and especially for mine unhappy daughter, which hath not seen any good at all in this world.

65 And the apostle, hearing these things from the captain, was greatly grieved for him, and said unto him: Believest thou that Jesus will heal them? And the captain said: Yea. And the apostle said: Commit thyself then unto Jesus, and he will heal them and procure them succour. And the captain said: Show me him, that I may entreat him and believe in him. And the apostle said: He appeareth not unto these bodily eyes, but is found by the eyes of the mind. The captain therefore lifted up his voice and said: I believe thee, Jesu, and entreat and supplicate thee, help my little faith which I have in thee. And the apostle commanded Xenophon (Syr. Xanthippus) the deacon to assemble all the brethren; and when the whole multitude was gathered, the apostle stood in the midst and said:

66 Children and brethren that have believed on the Lord, abide in this faith, preaching Jesus who was proclaimed unto you by me, to bring you hope in him; and forsake not (be not forsaken of) him, and he will not forsake you. While ye sleep in this slumber that weigheth down the sleepers, he, sleeping not, keepeth watch over you; and when ye sail and are in peril and none can help, he walking upon the waters supporteth and aideth. For I am now departing from you, and it appeareth not if I shall

again see you according to the flesh. Be ye not therefore like unto the people of Israel, who losing sight of their pastors for an hour, stumbled. But I leave unto you Xenophon the deacon in my stead; for he also like myself proclaimeth Jesus: for neither am I aught, nor he, but Jesus only; for I also am a man clothed with a body, a son of man like one of you; for neither have I riches as it is found with some, which also convict them that possess them, being wholly useless, and left behind upon the earth, whence also they came, and they bear away with them the transgressions and blemishes of sins which befall men by their means. And scantly are rich men found in almsgivillg: but the merciful and lowly in heart, these shall inherit the kingdom of God: for it is not beauty that endureth with men, for they that trust in it, when age cometh upon them, shall suddenly be put to shame: all things therefore have their time; in their season are they loved and hated. Let your hope then be in Jesus Christ the Son of God, which is always loved, and always desired: and be mindful of us, as we of you: for we too, if we fulfil not the burden of the commandments are not worthy to be preachers of this name, and hereafter shall we pay the price (punishment) of our own head.

67 And he prayed with them and continued with them a long time in prayer and supplication, and committing them unto the Lord, he said: O Lord that rulest over every soul that is in the body; Lord, Father of the souls that have their hope in thee and expect thy mercies: that redeemest from error the men that are thine own and settest free from bondage and corruption thy subjects that come unto thy refuge: be thou in the flock of Xenophon and anoint it with holy oil, and heal it of sores, and preserve it from the ravening wolves. And he laid his hand on them and said: The peace of the Lord shall be upon you and shall journey with us.

THE EIGHTH ACT

Of the wild asses

68 The apostle therefore went forth to depart on the way: and they all escorted him, weeping and adjuring him to make remembrance of them in his prayers and not to forget them. He went up then and sat upon the

chariot, leaving all the brethren, and the captain came and awaked the driver, saying: I entreat and pray that I may become worthy to sit beneath his feet, and I will be his driver upon this way, that he also may become my guide in that way whereby few go.

69 And when they had journeyed about two miles, the apostle begged of the captain and made him arise and caused him to sit by him, suffering the driver to sit in his own place. And as they went along the road, it came to pass that the beasts were wearied with the great heat and could not be stirred at all. And the captain was greatly vexed and wholly cast down, and thought to run on his own feet and bring other beasts for the use of the chariot; but the apostle said: Let not thine heart be troubled nor affrighted, but believe on Jesus Christ whom I have proclaimed unto thee, and thou shalt see great wonders. And he looked and saw a herd of wild asses feeding by the wayside, and said to the captain: If thou hast believed on Christ Jesus, go unto that herd of wild asses and say: Judas Thomas the apostle of Christ the new God saith unto you: Let four of you come, of whom we have need (or, of whom we may have use).

70 And the captain went in fear, for they were many; and as he went, they came to meet him; and when they were near, he said unto them: Judas Thomas the apostle of the new God commandeth you: Let four of you come, of whom I have need. And when the wild asses heard it, they ran with one accord and came to him, and when they came they did him reverence. [Syr. has a long prayer: And Judas Thomas the apostle of our Lord lifted up his voice in praise and said: Glorious art thou, God of truth and Lord of all natures, for thou didst will with thy will, and make all thy works and finish all thy creatures, and bring them to the rule of their nature, and lay upon them all thy fear that they might be subject to thy command. And thy will trod the path from thy secrecy to manifestation, and was caring for every soul that thou didst make, and was spoken of by the mouth of all the prophets, in all visions and sounds and voices; but Israel did not obey because of their evil inclination. And thou, because thou art Lord of all, hast a care for the creatures, so that thou spreadest over us thy mercy in him who came by thy will and put on the body, thy creature, which thou didst will and form according to thy glorious wisdom. He whom thou didst appoint in thy secrecy and establish in thy manifestation, to him thou hast given the name of Son, he who was thy will, the power of thy thought; so that ye are by various names, the Father and the Son and the Spirit, for the sake of the government of thy creatures,

for the nourishing of all natures, and ye are one in glory and power and will; and ye are divided without being separated, and are one though divided, and all subsists in thee and is subject to thee, because all is thine. And I rely upon thee, Lord, and by thy command have subjected these dumb beasts, that thou mightest show thy ministering power upon us and upon them because it is needful, and that thy name might be glorified in us and in the beasts that cannot speak.] And the apostle said unto them: Peace be unto you. Yoke ye four of you in the stead of these beasts that have come to a stand. And every one of them came and pressed to be yoked: there were then four stronger than the rest, which also were yoked. And the rest, some went before and some followed. And when they had journeyed a little way he dismissed the colts, saying: I say unto you the inhabiters of the desert, depart unto your pastures, for if I had had need of all, ye would all have gone with me; but now go unto your place wherein ye dwell. And they departed quietly until they were no more seen.

71 Now as the apostle and the captain and the driver went on, the wild asses drew the chariot quietly and evenly, lest they should disturb the apostle of God. And when they came near to the city gate they turned aside and stood still before the doors of the captain's house. And the captain said: It is not possible for me to relate what hath happened, but when I see the end I will tell it. The whole city therefore came to see the wild asses under the yoke; and they had heard also the report of the apostle that he was to come and visit them. And the apostle asked the captain: Where is thy dwelling, and whither dost thou bring us? And he said to him: Thou thyself knowest that we stand before the doors, and these which by thy commandment are come with thee know it better than I.

72 And having so said he came down from the chariot. The apostle therefore began to say: Jesu Christ, that art blasphemed by the ignorance of thee in this country; Jesu, the report of whom is strange in this city; Jesu, that receivest all (Syr. sendest on before the apostles in every country and in every city, and all thine that are worthy are glorified in thee; Jesu, that didst take a form and become as a man, and wert seen of all us that thou mightest not separate us from thine own love: thou, Lord, art he that gavest thyself for us, and with thy blood hast purchased us and gained us as a possession of great price: and what have we to give thee, Lord, in exchange for thy life which thou gavest for us? for that which we would give, thou gavest us: and this is, that we should entreat of thee and live.

73 And when he had so said, many assembled from every quarter to

see the apostle of the new God. And again the apostle said: Why stand we idle? Jesu, Lord, the hour is come: what wilt thou have done? command therefore that that be fulfilled which needeth to be done. Now the captain's wife and her daughter were sore borne down by the devils, so that they of the house thought they would rise up no more: for they suffered them not to partake of aught, but cast them down upon their beds recognizing no man until that day when the apostle came thither. And the apostle said unto one of the wild asses that were yoked on the right hand: Enter thou within the gate, and stand there and call the devils and say to them: Judas Thomas the apostle and disciple of Jesus Christ saith unto you: Come forth hither: for on your account am I sent and unto them that pertain to you by race, to destroy you and chase you unto your place, until the time of the end come and ye go down into your own deep of darkness.

74 And that wild ass went in, a great multitude being with him, and said: Unto you I speak, the enemies of Jesus that is called Christ: unto you I speak that shut your eyes lest ye see the light: unto you I speak, children of Gehenna and of destruction, of him that ceaseth not from evil until now, that always reneweth his workings and the things that befit his being: unto you I speak, most shameless, that shall perish by your own hands. And what I shall say of your destruction and end, and what I shall tell, I know not. For there are many things and innumerable to the hearing: and greater are your doings than the torment that is reserved for you (Syr. however great your bodies, they are too small for your retributions). But unto thee I speak, devil, and to thy son that followeth with thee: for now am I sent against you. And wherefore should I make many words concerning your nature and root, which yourselves know and are not ashamed? but Judas Thomas the apostle of Christ Jesus saith unto you, he that by much love and affection is sent hither: Before all this multitude that standeth here, come forth and tell me of what race ye are.

75 And straightway the woman came forth with her daughter, both like dead persons and dishonoured in aspect: and the apostle beholding them was grieved. especially for the girl, and saith unto the devils: God forbid that for you there should be sparing or propitiation, for ye know not to spare nor to have pity: but in the name of Jesus, depart from them and stand by their side. And when the apostle had so said, the women fell down and became as dead; for they neither had breath nor uttered speech: but the devil answered with a loud voice and said: Art thou come hither again, thou that deridest our nature and race? art thou come again, that

blottest out our devices? and as I take it, thou wouldest not suffer us to be upon the earth at all: but this at this time thou canst not accomplish. And the apostle guessed that this devil was he that had been driven out from that other woman.

76 And the devil said: I beseech thee, give me leave to depart even whither thou wilt, and dwell there and take commandment from thee, and I will not fear the ruler that hath authority over me. For like as thou art come to preach good tidings, so I also am come to destroy; and like as, if thou fulfil not the will of him that sent thee, he will bring punishment upon thy head, so I also if I do not the will of him that sent me, before the season and time appointed, shall be sent unto mine own nature; and like as thy Christ helpeth thee in that thou doest, so also my father helpeth me in that I do; and like as for thee he prepareth vessels worthy of thine inhabiting, so also for me he seeketh out vessels whereby I may accomplish his deeds; and like as he nourisheth and provideth for his subjects, so also for me he prepareth chastisements and torments, with them that become my dwellingplaces (Syr. those in whom I dwell); and like as for a recompense of thy working he giveth thee eternal life, so also unto me he giveth for a reward of my works eternal destruction; and like as thou art refreshed by thy prayer and thy good works and spiritual thanksgivings, so I also am refreshed by murders and adulteries and sacrifices made with wine upon altars (Syr. sacrifices and libations of wine), and like as thou convertest men unto eternal life, so I also pervert them that obey me unto eternal destruction and torment: and thou receivest thine own and I mine.

77 And when the devil had said these things and yet more the apostle said: Jesus commandeth thee and thy son by me to enter no more into the habitation of man: but go ye forth and depart and dwell wholly apart from the habitation of men. And the devils said unto him: Thou hast laid on us a harsh commandment: but what wilt thou do unto them that now are concealed from thee? for they that have wrought all the images rejoice in them more than thee: and many of them do the more part worship, and perform their will, sacrificing to them and bringing them food, by libations and by wine and water and offering with oblations. And the apostle said: They also shall now be abolished, with their works. And suddenly the devils vanished away: but the women lay cast upon the earth as if were dead, and without speech.

78 And the wild asses stood together and parted not one from another; but he to whom speech was given by the power of the Lord -while all men

kept silence, and looked to see what they would do- the wild ass said unto the apostle: Why standest thou idle, O apostle of Christ the Most High, who looketh that thou shouldest ask of him the best of learning? Wherefore then tarriest thou? (Syr. that thou shouldest ask him, and he would give thee? Why delayest thou, good disciple?) for lo, thy teacher desireth to show by thy hands his mighty works. Why standest thou still, O herald of the hidden one? for thy (Lord) willeth to manifest through thee his unspeakable things, which he reserveth for them that are worthy of him, to hear them. Why restest thou, O doer of mighty works in the name of the Lord? for thy Lord encourageth thee and engendereth boldness in thee. Fear not, therefore; for he will not forsake the soul that belongeth unto thee by birth. Begin therefore to call upon him and he will readily hearken to thee. Why standest thou marvelling at all his acts and his workings? for these are small things which he hath shown by thy means. And what wilt thou tell concerning his great gifts? for thou wilt not be sufficient to declare them. And why marvellest thou at his cures of the body which he worketh? (Syr. which come to an end) especially when thou knowest that healing of his which is secure and lasting, which he bringeth forth by his own nature? And why lookest thou unto this temporal life, and hast no thought of that which is eternal (Syr. when thou canst every day think on that which is eternal)?

79 But unto you the multitudes that stand by and look to see these that are cast down raised up, I say, believe in the apostle of Jesus Christ: believe the teacher of truth, believe him that showeth you the truth, believe Jesus, believe on the Christ that was born, that the born may live by his life: who also was raised up through infancy, that perfection might appear by his manhood (man). He did teach his own disciples: for he is the teacher of the truth and maketh wise men wise (Syr. who went to school that through him perfect wisdom might be known: he taught his teacher because he was the teacher of verity and the master of the wise). Who also offered the gift in the temple that he might show that all the (every) offering was sanctified. This is his apostle, the shewer-forth of truth: this is he that performeth the will of him that sent him. But there shall come false apostles and prophets of lawlessness, whose end shall be according to their deeds; preaching indeed and ordaining to flee from ungodliness, but themselves at all times detected in sins, clad indeed with sheep's clothing, but within, ravening wolves. Who suffice not themselves with one wife but corrupt many women; who, saying that they

despise children, destroy many children (boys), for whom they will pay the penalty; that content not themselves with their own possessions, but desire that all useless things should minister unto them only; professing to be his disciples; and with their mouth they utter one thing, but in their heart they think another; charging other men to beware of evil, but they themselves perform nought that is good; who are accounted temperate, and charge other men to abstain from fornication theft, and covetousness, but in all these things do they themselves walk secretly, teaching other men not to do them.

80 And when the wild ass had declared all these things, all men gazed upon him. And when he ceased the apostle said: What I shall think concerning thy beauty, O Jesu, and what I shall tell of thee, I know not, or rather I am not able, for I have no power to declare it, O Christ that art in rest, and only wise that only knowest the inward of the heart and understandest the thought. Glory be to thee, merciful and tranquil. Glory to thee, wise word. Glory to thy compassion that was born unto us. Glory to thy mercy that was spread out over us. Glory to thy greatness that was made small for us. Glory to thy most high kingship that was humbled for us. Glory to thy might which was enfeebled for us. Glory to thy Godhead that for us was seen in likeness of men. Glory to thy manhood that died for us that it might make us live. Glory to thy resurrection from the dead; for thereby rising and rest cometh unto our souls. Glory and praise (good report) to thine ascending into the heavens; for thereby thou hast shewed us the path of the height, and promised that we shall sit with thee on thy right hand and with thee judge the twelve tribes of Israel. Thou art the heavenly word of the Father: thou art the hidden light of the understanding, shewer of the way of truth, driver away of darkness, and blotter-out of error.

81 Having thus spoken, the apostle stood over the women, saying: My Lord and my God, I am not divided from thee (or doubt not concerning thee), nor as one unbelieving do I call upon thee, who art always our helper and succourer and raiser-up; who breathest thine own power into us and encouragest us and givest confidence in love unto thine own servants. I beseech thee, let these souls be healed and rise up and become such as they were before they were smitten of the devils. And when he thus spake the women turned and sat up. And the apostle bade the captain that his servants should take them and bring them within (Syr. and give them food, for they had not eaten for many days). And when they were gone in, the apostle said unto the wild asses, Follow me. And they went

after him until he had brought them without the gate. And when they had gone out, he said to them: Depart in peace unto your pastures. The wild asses therefore went away willingly; and the apostle stood and took heed to them lest they should be hurt of any, until they had gone afar off and were no more seen. And the apostle returned with the multitude into the house of the captain.

THE NINTH ACT

Of the Wife of Charisius

82 Now it chanced that a certain woman, the wife of Charisius, that was next unto the king, whose name was Mygdonia, came to see and behold the new name and the new God who was being proclaimed, and the new apostle who had come to visit their country: and she was carried by her own servants; and because of the great crowd and the narrow way they were not able to bring her near unto him. And she sent unto her husband to send her more to minister to her; and they came and approached her, pressing upon the people and beating them. And the apostle saw it and said to them: Wherefore overthrow ye them that come to hear the word, and are eager for it? and ye desire to be near me but are far off, as it was said of the multitude that came unto the Lord: Having eyes ye see not, and having ears ye hear not; and he said to the multitudes: He that hath ears to hear, let him hear; and: Come unto me, all ye that labour and are heavy laden, and I will give you rest.

83 And looking upon them that carried her, he said unto them: This blessing and this admonition [Here and elsewhere there is a marked divergence between the texts of U and P, the Roman and Paris MSS.: Bonnet prints them separately. P is on the whole much shorter. Syr. differs from both. I follow U, but it is very corrupt.] which was promised unto them is for you that are heavily burdened now. Ye are they that carry burdens grievous to be borne, and are borne about by her command. And though ye are men, they lay on you loads as on brute beasts, for they that have authority over you think that ye are not men such as themselves, whether bond or free. For neither shall possessions profit the rich, nor poverty save the poor

from judgement; nor have we received a commandment which we are not able to perform, nor hath he laid on us burdens grievous to be borne which we are not able to carry; nor building which men build; nor to hew stones and prepare houses, as your craftsmen do by their own knowledge. But this commandment have we received of the Lord, that that which pleaseth not us when it is done by another this we should not do to any other man.

84 Abstain therefore first from adultery, for this is the beginning of all evils, and next from theft, which enticed Judas Iscariot, and brought him unto hanging; (and from covetousness,) for as many as yield unto covetousness see not that which they do; and from vainglory and from all foul deeds, especially them of the body, whereby cometh eternal condemnation. For this is the chief city of all evils; and likewise it bringeth them that hold their heads (necks) high unto tyranny, and draweth them down unto the deep, and subdueth them under its hands that they see not what they do; wherefore the things done of them are hidden from them.

85 But do ye become well-pleasing unto God in all good things, in meekness and quietness: for these doth God spare, and granteth eternal life and setteth death at nought. And in gentleness which followeth on all good things, and overcometh all enemies and alone receiveth the crown of victory: with gentleness (Syr.), and stretching out of the hand to the poor, and supplying the want of the needy, and distributing to them that are in necessity, especially them that walk in holiness. For this is chosen before God and leadeth unto eternal life: for this is before God the chief city of all good: for they that strive not in the course (stadium) of Christ shall not obtain holiness. And holiness did appear from God, doing away fornication, overthrowing the enemy, well-pleasing unto God: for she is an invincible champion (athlete), having honour from God, glorified of many: she is an ambassador of peace, announcing peace: if any gain her he abideth without care, pleasing the Lord, expecting the time of redemption: for she doeth nothing amiss, but giveth life and rest and joy unto all that gain her. [P has nothing of this, and Syr. makes better sense, but is not very interesting.]

86 But meekness hath overcome death and brought him under authority, meekness hath enslaved the enemy [U and P and Syr. now present the same text], meekness is the good yoke: meekness feareth not and opposeth not the many: meekness is peace and joy and exaltation of rest. Abide ye therefore in holiness and receive freedom from me, and be near unto meekness for in these three heads is portrayed the Christ whom I proclaim

unto you. Holiness is the temple of Christ, and he that dwelleth in her getteth her for an habitation [Syr. is the of God rest temperance and], because for forty days and forty nights he fasted, tasting nothing: and he that keepeth her shall dwell in her as on a mountain. And meekness is his boast: for he said unto Peter our fellow apostle: Turn back thy sword and put it again into the sheath thereof: for if I had willed so to do, could I not have brought more than twelve legions of angels from my Father?

87 And when the apostle had said these things in the hearing of all the multitude, they trode and pressed upon one another: and the wife of Charisius the king's kinsman leapt out of her chair and cast herself on the earth before the apostle, and caught his feet and besought and said: O disciple of the living God, thou art come into a desert country, for we live in the desert; being like to brute beasts in our conversation, but now shall we be saved by thy hands; I beseech thee, therefore, take thought of me, and pray for me, that the compassion of the God whom thou preachest may come upon me, and I may become his dwelling place and be joined in prayer and hope and faith in him, and I also may receive the seal and become an holy temple and he may dwell in me.

88 And the apostle said: I do pray and entreat for you all, brethren, that believe on the Lord, and for you, sisters, that hope in Christ, that in all of you the word of God may tabernacle and have his tabernacle therein: for we have no power over them (Syr. because ye are given power over your own souls). And he began to say unto the woman Mygdonia: Rise up from the earth and compose thyself (take off thine ornaments, P; be mindful of thyself, Syr.). For this attire that is put on shall not profit thee nor the beauty of thy body, nor thine apparel, neither yet the fame of thy rank, nor the authority of this world, nor the polluted intercourse with thine husband shall avail thee if thou be bereaved of the true fellowship: for the appearance (fantasy) of ornamenting cometh to nought, and the body waxeth old and changeth, and raiment weareth out, and authority and lordship pass away (U corrupt; P abridges; Syr. has: passeth away accompanied with punishment, according as each person hath conducted himself in it), and the fellowship of procreation also passeth away, and is as it were condemnation. Jesus only abideth ever, and they that hope in him. Thus he spake, and said unto the woman: Depart in peace, and the Lord shall make thee worthy of his own mysteries. But she said: I fear to go away, lest thou forsake me and depart unto another nation. But the apostle said to her: Even if I go, I shall not leave thee alone, but

Jesus of his compassion will be with thee. And she fell down and did him reverence and departed unto her house.

89 Now Charisius, the kinsman of Misdaeus the king, bathed himself and returned and laid him down to dine. And he inquired concerning his wife, where she was; for she had not come out of her own chamber to meet him as she was wont. And her handmaids said to him: She is not well. And he entered quickly into the chamber and found her Lying on the bed and veiled: and he unveiled her and kissed her, saying: Wherefore art thou sorrowful to-day? And she said: I am not well. And he said unto her: Wherefore then didst thou not keep the guise of thy freedom (Syr. pay proper respect to thy position as a free woman) and remain in thy house, but didst go and listen unto vain speeches and look upon works of sorcery? but rise up and dine with me, for I cannot dine without thee. But she said to him: To-day I decline it, for I am greatly afeared.

90 And when Charisius heard this of Mygdonia, he would not go forth to dinner, but bade his servants bring her to dine with him (Syr. bring food to him that he might sup in her presence): when then they brought it in, he desired her to dine with him, but she excused herself; since then she would not, he dined alone, saying unto her: On thine account I refused to dine with Misdaeus the king, and thou, wast thou not willing to dine with me? but she said: It is because I am not well. Charisius therefore rose up as he was wont and would sleep with her, but she said: Did I not tell thee that for today I refused it?

91 When he heard that he went to another bed and slept; and awaking out of sleep he said: My lady Mygdonia, hearken to the dream which I have seen. I saw myself lie at meat near to Misdaeus the king, and a dish of all sorts was set before us: and I saw an eagle come down from heaven and carry off from before me and the king two partridges, which he set against his heart; and again he came over us and flew about above us, and the king bade a bow to be brought to him; and the eagle again caught away from before us a pigeon and a dove, and the king shot an arrow at him, and it passed through him from one side to the other and hurt him not; and he being unscathed rose up into his own nest. And I awoke, and I am full of fear and sore vexed, because I had tasted of the partridge, and he suffered me not to put it to my mouth again. And Mygdonia said unto him: Thy dream is good: for thou every day eatest partridges, but this eagle had not tasted of a partridge until now.

92 And when it was morning Charisius went and dressed himself

and shod his right foot with his left shoe; and he stopped, and said to Mygdonia: What then is this matter? for look, the dream and this action of mine! But Mygdonia said to him: And this also is not evil, but seemeth to me very good; for from an unlucky act there will be a change unto the better. And he washed his hands and went to salute Misdaeus the king.

93 And likewise Mygdonia rose up early and went to salute Judas Thomas the apostle, and she found him discoursing with the captain and all the multitude, and he was advising them and speaking of the woman which had received the Lord in her soul, whose wife she was; and the captain said: She is the wife of Charisius the kinsman of Misdaeus the king. And: Her husband is a hard man, and in every thing that he saith to the king he obeyeth him: and he will not suffer her to continue in this mind which she hath promised; for often-times hath he praised her before the king, saying that there is none other like her in love: all things therefore that thou speakest unto her are strange unto her. And the apostle said: If verily and surely the Lord hath risen upon her soul and she hath received the seed that was cast on her, she will have no care of this temporal life, nor fear death, neither will Charisius be able to harm her at all: for greater is he whom she hath received into her soul, if she have received him indeed.

94 And Mygdonia hearing this said unto the apostle: In truth, my lord, I have received the seed of thy words, and I will bear fruit like unto such seed. The apostle saith: Our souls give praise and thanks unto thee, O Lord, for they are thine: our bodies give thanks unto thee, which thou hast accounted worthy to become the dwelling-place of thy heavenly gift. And he said also to them that stood by: Blessed are the holy, whose souls have never condemned them, for they have gained them and are not divided against themselves: blessed are the spirits of the pure, and they that have received the heavenly crown whole from the world (age) which hath been appointed them: blessed are the bodies of the holy, for they have been made worthy to become temples of God, that Christ may dwell in them: blessed are ye, for ye have power to forgive sins: blessed are ye if ye lose not that which is committed unto you, but rejoicing and departing bear it away with you: blessed are ye the holy, for unto you it is given to ask and receive: blessed are ye meek for you hath God counted worthy to become heirs of the heavenly kingdom. Blessed are ye meek, for ye are they that have overcome the enemy: blessed are ye meek, for ye shall see the face of the Lord. Blessed are ye that hunger for the Lord's sake for for you is

rest laid up, and your souls rejoice from henceforth. Blessed are ye that are quiet, (for ye have been counted worthy) to be set free from sin [and from the exchange of clean and unclean beasts]. And when the apostle had said these things in the hearing of all the multitude, Mygdonia was the more confirmed in the faith and glory and greatness of Christ.

95 But Charisius the kinsman and friend of Misdaeus the king came to his breakfast and found not his wife in the house; and he inquired of all that were in his house: Whither is your mistress gone? And one of them answered and said: She is gone unto that stranger. And when he heard this of his servant, he was wroth with the other servants because they had not straightway told him what was done: and he sat down and waited for her. And when it was evening and she was come into the house he said to her: Where wast thou? And she answered and said: With the physician. And he said: Is that stranger a physician? And she said: Yea, he is a physician of souls: for most physicians do heal bodies that are dissolved, but he souls that are not destroyed. Charisius, hearing this, was very angry in his mind with Mygdonia because of the apostle, but he answered her nothing, for he was afraid; for she was above him both in wealth and birth: but he departed to dinner, and she went into her chamber. And he said to the servants: Call her to dinner. But she would not come.

96 And when he heard that she would not come out of her chamber, he went in and said unto her: Wherefore wilt thou not dine with me and perchance not sleep with me as the wont is? yea, concerning this I have the greater suspicion, for I have heard that that sorcerer and deceiver teacheth that a man should not live with his wife, and that which nature requireth and the godhead hath ordained he overthroweth. When Charisius said these things, Mygdonia kept silence. He saith to her again: My lady and consort Mygdonia, be not led astray by deceitful and vain words, nor by the works of sorcery which I have heard that this man performeth in the name of Father, Son, and Holy Ghost; for it was never yet heard in the world that any raised the dead, and, as I hear, it is reported of this man that he raiseth dead men. And for that he neither eateth nor drinketh, think not that for righteousness sake he neither eateth nor drinketh but this he doth because he possesseth nought, for what should he do which hath not even his daily bread? And he hath one garment because he is poor, and as for his not receiving aught of any (he doth so, to be sure, because he knoweth in himself that he doth not verily heal any man, Syr.).

97 And when Charisius so said, Mygdonia was silent as any stone, but

she prayed, asking when it should be day, that she might go to the apostle of Christ. And he withdrew from her and went to dinner heavy in mind, for he thought to sleep with her according to the wont. And when he was gone out, she bowed her knees and prayed, saying: Lord God and Master, merciful Father, Saviour Christ, do thou give me strength to overcome the shamelessness of Charisius, and grant me to keep the holiness wherein thou delightest, that I also may by it find eternal life. And when she had so prayed she laid herself on her bed and veiled herself.

98 But Charisius having dined came upon her, and she cried out, saying: Thou hast no more any room by me: for my Lord Jesus is greater than thou, who is with me and resteth in me. And he laughed and said: Well dost thou mock, saying this of that sorcerer, and well dost thou deride him, who saith: Ye have no life with God unless ye purify yourselves. And when he had so said he essayed to sleep with her, but she endured it not and cried out bitterly and said: I call upon thee, Lord Jesu, forsake me not! for with thee have I made my refuge; for when I learned that thou art he that seekest out them that are veiled in ignorance and savest them that are held in error And now I entreat thee whose report I have heard and believed, come thou to my help and save me from the shamelessness of Charisius, that his foulness may not get the upper hand of me. And she smote her hands together (tied his hands, Syr.) and fled from him naked, and as she went forth she pulled down the curtain of the bed-chamber and wrapped it about her; and went to her nurse, and slept there with her.

99 But Charisius was in heaviness all night, and smote his face with his hands, and he was minded to go that very hour and tell the king concerning the violence that was done him, but he considered with himself, saying: If the great heaviness which is upon me compelleth me to go now unto the king, who will bring me in to him? for I know that my abuse hath overthrown me from my high looks and my vainglory and majesty, and hath cast me down into this vileness and separated my sister Mygonia from me. Yea, if the king himself stood before the doors at this hour, I could not have gone out and answered him. But I will wait until dawn, and I know that whatsoever I ask of the king, he granteth it me: and I will tell him of the madness of this stranger, how that it tyrannously casteth down the great and illustrious into the depth. For it is not this that grieveth me, that I am deprived of her companying, but for her am I grieved, because her greatness of soul is humbled: being an honourable lady in whom none of her house ever found fault (condemned), she hath fled away naked,

running out of her own bedchamber, and I know not whither she is gone; and it may be that she is gone mad by the means of that sorcerer, and in her madness hath gone forth into the market-place to seek him; for there is nothing that appealeth unto her lovable except him and the things that are spoken by him.

100 And so saving he began to lament and say: Woe to me, O my consort, and to thee besides! for I am too quickly bereaved of thee. Woe is me, my most dear one, for thou excellest all my race: neither son nor daughter have I had of thee that I might find rest in them; neither hast thou yet dwelt with me a full year, and an evil eye hath caught thee from me. Would that the violence of death had taken thee, and I should yet have reckoned myself among kings and nobles: but that I should suffer this at the hands of a stranger, and belike he is a slave that hath run away, to mine ill fortune and the sorrow of mine unhappy soul! Let there be no impediment for me until I destroy him and avenge this night, and may I not be well-pleasing before Misdaeus the king if he avenge me not with the head of this stranger; (and I will also tell him) of Siphor the captain who hath been the occasion of this. For by his means did the stranger appear here, and lodgeth at his house: and many there be that go in and come out whom he teacheth a new doctrine; saying that none can live if he quit not all his substance and become a renouncer like himself: and he striveth to make many partakers with him.

101 And as Charisius thought on these things, the day dawned: and after the night (?) he put on a mean habit, and shod himself, and went downcast and in heaviness to salute the king. And when the king saw him he said: Wherefore art thou sorrowful, and comest in such garb? and I see that thy countenance is changed. And Charisius said unto the king: I have a new thing to tell thee and a new desolation which Siphor hath brought into India, even a certain Hebrew, a sorcerer, whom he hath sitting in his house and who departeth not from him: and many are there that go in to him: whom also he teacheth of a new God, and layeth on them new laws such as never yet were heard, saving: It is impossible for you to enter into that eternal life which I proclaim unto you, unless ye rid you of your wives, and likewise the wives of their husbands. And it chanced that mine unlucky wife also went to him and became a hearer of his words, and she believed them, and in the night she forsook me and ran unto the stranger. But send thou for both Siphor and that sorcerer that is hid with (in) him, and visit it (?) on their head, lest all that are of our nation perish.

102 And when Misdaeus his friend heard this he saith to him: Be not grieved nor heavy, for I will send for him and avenge thee, and thou shalt have thy wife again, and the others that cannot I will avenge. And the king went forth and sat on the judgement seat, and when he was set he commanded Siphor the captain to be called. They went therefore unto his house and found him sitting on the right hand of the apostle and Mygdonia at his feet, hearkening to him with all the multitude. And they that were sent from the king said unto Siphor: Sittest thou here listening to vain words, and Misdaeus the king in his wrath thinketh to destroy thee because of this sorcerer and deceiver whom thou hast brought into thine house? And Siphor hearing it was cast down, not because of the king's threat against him, but for the apostle, because the king was disposed contrary to him. And he said to the apostle: I am grieved concerning thee: for I told thee at the first that that woman is the wife of Charisius the king's friend and kinsman, and he will not suffer her to perform that she hath promised, and all that he asketh of the king he granteth him. But the apostle said unto Siphor: Fear nothing, but believe in Jesus that pleadeth for us all, for unto his refuge are we gathered together. And Siphor, hearing that, put his garment about him and went unto Misdaeus the king,

103 And the apostle inquired of Mygdonia: What was the cause that thy husband was wroth with thee and devised this against us? And she said: Because I gave not myself up unto his corruption (destruction): for he desired last night to subdue me and subject me unto that passion which he serveth: and he to whom I have committed my soul delivered me out of his hands; and I fled away from him naked, and slept with my nurse: but that which befell him I know not, wherefore he hath contrived this. The apostle saith: These things will not hurt us; but believe thou on Jesus, and he shall overthrow the wrath of Charisius and his madness and his impulse; and he shall be a companion unto thee in the fearful way, and he shall guide thee into his kingdom, and shall bring thee unto eternal life giving thee that confidence which passeth not away nor changeth.

104 Now Siphor stood before the king, and he inquired of him: Who is that sorcerer and whence, and what teacheth he whom thou hast lurking in thine house? And Siphor answered the king: Thou art not ignorant, O king, what trouble and grief I, with my friends had concerning my wife, whom thou knowest and many others remember, and concerning my daughter, whom I value more than all my possessions, what a time and trial I suffered; for I became a laughing-stock and a curse in all our

country. And I heard the report of this man and went to him and entreated him, and took him and brought him hither. And as I came by the way I saw wonderful and amazing things: and here also many did hear the wild ass and concerning that devil whom he drove out, and healed my wife and daughter, and now are they whole; and he asked no reward but requireth faith and holiness, that men should become partakers with him in that which he doeth: and this he teacheth to worship and fear one God, the ruler of all things, and Jesus Christ his Son, that they may have eternal life. And that which he eateth is bread and salt, and his drink is water from evening unto evening, and he maketh many prayers; and whatsoever he asketh of his God, he giveth him. And he teacheth that this God is holy and mighty, and that Christ is living and maketh alive, wherefore also he chargeth them that are there present to come unto him in holiness and purity and love and faith.

105 And when Misdaeus the king heard these things of Siphor he sent many soldiers unto the house of Siphor the captain, to bring Thomas the apostle and all that were found there. And they that were sent entered in and found him teaching much people; and Mygdonia sat at his feet. And when they beheld the great multitude that were about him, they feared, and departed to their king and said: We durst not say aught unto him, for there was a great multitude about him, and Mygdonia sitting at his feet was listening to the things that were spoken by him. And when Misdaeus the king and Charisius heard these things, Charisius leaped out from before the king and drew much people with him and said: I will bring him, O king, and Mygdonia whose understanding he hath taken away. And he came to the house of Siphor the captain, greatly disturbed, and found him (Thomas) teaching: but Mygdonia he found not, for she had withdrawn herself unto her house, having learnt that it had been told her husband that she was there.

106 And Charisius said unto the apostle: Up, thou wicked one and destroyer and enemy of mine house: for me thy sorcery harmeth not, for I will visit thy sorcery on thine head. And when he so said, the apostle looked upon him and said unto him: Thy threatenings shall return upon thee, for me thou wilt not harm any whit: for greater than thee and thy king and all your army is the Lord Jesus Christ in whom I have my trust. And Chalisius took a kerchief (turban, Syr.) of one of his slaves and cast it about the neck of the apostle, saying: Hale him and bring him away; let me see if his God is able to deliver him out of my hands. And they

82

haled him and led him away to Misdaeus the king. And the apostle stood before the king, and the king said to him: Tell me who thou art and by what power thou doest these things. But the apostle kept silence. And the king commanded his officers (subjects) that he should be scourged with an hundred and twenty-eight (hundred and fifty, Syr.) blows, and bound, and be cast into the prison; and they bound him and led him away. And the king and Charisius considered how they should put him to death, for the multitude worshipped him as God. And they had it in mind to say: The stranger hath reviled the king and is a deceiver.

107 But the apostle went unto the prison rejoicing and exulting, and said: I praise thee, Jesu, for that thou hast not only made me worthy of faith in thee, but also to endure much for thy sake. I give thee thanks therefore, Lord, that thou hast taken thought for me and given me patience: I thank thee Lord, that for thy sake I am called a sorcerer and a wizard. Receive thou me therefore with the blessing (Syr. let me receive of the blessing) of the poor, and of the rest of the weary, and of the blessings of them whom men hate and persecute and revile, and speak evil words of them. For lo, for thy sake I am hated: lo for thy sake I am cut off from the many, and for thy sake they call me such an one as I am not.

108 And as he prayed, all the prisoners looked on him, and besought him to pray for them: and when he had prayed and was set down, he began to utter a psalm in this wise:

[Here follows the Hymn of the Soul: a most remarkable composition, originally Syriac, and certainly older than the Acts, with which it has no real connection. We have it in Greek in one manuscript, the Vallicellian, and in a paraphrase by Nicetas of Thessalonica, found and edited by Bonnet.]

When I was an infant child in the palace of my Father and resting in the wealth and luxury of my nurturers, out of the East, our native country, my parents provisioned me and sent me.

And of the wealth of those their treasures they put together a load both great and light, that I might carry it alone.

Gold is the load, of them that are above (or of the land of the Ellaeans or Gilaeans), and silver of the great treasures (or of Gazzak the great) and stones, chalcedonies from the Indians and pearls from [THE land of] the Kosani (Kushan).

And they armed me with adamant [WHICH iron breaketh] and they took off from me (Gr. put on me) the garment set with gems, spangled with gold, which they had made for me because they loved me and the robe that was yellow in hue, made for my stature.

And they made a covenant with me, and inscribed it on mine understanding, that I should [NOT] forget it, and said:

If thou go down into Egypt, and bring back thence the one pearl which is there [IN the of sea midst] girt about by the devouring serpent thou shalt put on [AGAIN] the garment set with gems, and that robe whereupon it resteth (or which is thereon) and become with thy brother that is next unto us (Gr. of the well-remembered) an heir (Gr. herald) in our kingdom.

109. And I came out of the East by a road difficult and fearful, with two guides and I was untried in travelling by it.

And I passed by the borders of the Mosani (Maishan) where is the resort of the merchants of the East, and reached the land of the Babylonians [AND the of Sarbug walls unto came].

But when I entered into Egypt, the guides left me which had journeyed with me.

And I set forth by the quickest way to the serpent, and by his hole I abode watching for him to slumber and sleep, that I might take my pearl from him.

And forasmuch as I was alone I made mine aspect strange, and appeared as an alien to my people.

And there I saw my kinsman from the East, the free-born a lad of grace and beauty, a son of princes (or an anointed one).

He came unto me and dwelt with me, and I had him for a companion, and made him my friend and partaker in my journey (or merchandise).

And I charged him to beware of the Egyptians, and of partaking of those unclean things (or consorting with those unclean men).

And I put on their raiment, lest I should seem strange, as one that had come from without to recover the pearl; and lest the Egyptians should awake the serpent against me.

But, I know not by what occasion, they learned that I was not of their country.

And with guile they mingled for me a deceit, and I tasted of their food.

And I knew no more that I was a king's son, and I became a servant unto their king.

And I forgot also the pearl for which my fathers had sent me, and by means of the heaviness of their food I fell into a deep sleep.

110. But when this befell me, my fathers also were ware of it, and grieved for me and a proclamation was published in our kingdom, that all

should meet at our doors.

And then the kings of Parthia and they that bare office and the great ones of the East made a resolve concerning me, that I should not be left in Egypt, and the princes wrote unto me signifying thus (and every noble signed his name to it, Syr.):

From the (thy) Father the King of kings, and thy mother that ruleth the East, and thy brother that is second unto us; unto our son that is in Egypt, peace.

Rise up and awake out of sleep, and hearken unto the words of the letter and remember that thou art a son of kings; lo, thou hast come under the yoke of bondage.

Remember the pearl for the which thou wast sent into Egypt (Gr. puts this after 46).

Remember thy garment spangled with gold, [AND the and thyself deck shouldest thou wherewith wear which mantle glorious] Thy name is named in the book of life, and with thy brother whom thou hast received [THOU be shalt] in our kingdom.

111. [AND letter a was my] and the King [as ambassador] sealed it [WITH hand right his] because of the evil ones, even the children of the Babylonians and the tyrannous demons of Labyrinthus (Sarbug, Syr.).

It flew and lighted down by me, and became all speech.

And I at the voice of it and the feeling of it started up out of sleep and I took it up and kissed it [AND the seal brake] and read it.

And it was written concerning that which was recorded in mine heart.

And I remembered forthwith that I was a son of kings, and my freedom yearned (sought) after its kind.

I remembered also the pearl for the which I was sent down into Egypt and I began (or came) with charms against the terrible serpent, and I overcame him (or put him to sleep) by naming the name of my Father upon him, And I caught away the pearl and turned back to bear it unto my fathers.

And I stripped off the filthy garment and left it in their land, and directed my way forthwith to the light of my fatherland in the East.

And on the way I found my letter that had awakened me, and it, like as it had taken a voice and raised me when I slept, so also guided me with the light that came from it.

For at times the royal garment of silk [SHONE] before mine eyes, and with love leading me and drawing me onward, I passed by Labyrinthus

(Sarbug), and I left Babylon upon my left hand and I came unto Meson (Mesene; Maishan) the great, that lieth on the shore of the sea, from the heights of Warkan (Hyrcania?) had my parents sent thither by the hand of their treasurers, unto whom they committed it because of their faithfulness>.

112. But I remembered not the brightness of it; for I was yet a child and very young when I had left it in the palace of my Father, but suddenly, [when] I saw the garment made like unto me as it had been in a mirror.

And I beheld upon it all myself (or saw it wholly in myself) and I knew and saw myself through it, that we were divided asunder, being of one; and again were one in one shape.

Yea, the treasurers also which brought me the garment I beheld, that they were two, yet one shape was upon both, one royal sign was set upon both of them.

The money and the wealth had they in their hands, and paid me the due price, and the lovely garment, which was variegated with bright colours with gold and precious stones and pearls of comely hue they were fastened above (or in the height).

And the likeness of the King of kings was all in all of it. Sapphire stones were fitly set in it above (or, like the sapphire stone also were its manifold hues).

113. And again I saw that throughout it motions of knowledge were being sent forth, and it was ready to utter speech.

And I heard it speak:

I am of him that is more valiant than all men, for whose sake I was reared up with the Father himself.

And I also perceived his stature (so Gr.- Syr. I perceived in myself that my stature grew in accordance with his working).

And all its royal motions rested upon me as it grew toward the impulse of it (And with its kingly motions it was spreading itself toward me).

And it hastened, reaching out from the hand of [HIM it brought that] unto him that would receive it and me also did yearning arouse to start forth and meet it and receive it.

And I stretched forth and received it, and adorned myself with the beauty of the colours thereof (mostly Syr.; Gr. corrupt) and in my royal robe excelling in beauty I arrayed myself wholly.

And when I had put it on, I was lifted up unto the place of peace (sahltation) and homage and I bowed my head and worshipped the brightness of the Father which had sent it unto me. for I had performed his commandments, and he likewise that which he had promised, and at the doors of his palace which was from the beginning I mingled among, and he rejoiced over me and received me with him into his palace, and all his servants do praise him with sweet voices.

And he promised me that with him I shall be sent unto the gates of the king, that with my gifts and my pearl we may appear together before the king.

[Immediately on this, in the Syriac, follows a Song of Praise of Thomas the apostle consisting of forty-two ascriptions of praise and four final clauses (Wright, pp. 245-51). It has no bearing on the Acts, and is not in itself so remarkable as to need to be inserted here.]

114 And Charisius went home glad, thinking that his wife would be with him, and that she had become such as she was before, even before she heard the divine word and believed on Jesus. And he went, and found her with her hair dishevelled and her clothes rent, and when he saw it he said unto her: My lady Mygdonia, why doth this cruel disease keep hold on thee? and wherefore hast thou done this? I am thine husband from thy virginity, and both the gods and the law grant me to have rule over thee, what is this great madness of thine, that thou art become a derision in all our nation? but put thou away the care that cometh of that sorcerer; and I will remove his face from among us, that thou mayest see him no more.

115 But Mygdonia when she heard that gave herself up unto grief, groaning and lamenting and Charisius said again; Have I then so much wronged the gods that they have afflicted me with such a disease? what is my great offence that they have cast me into such humiliation? I beseech thee. Mvgdonia trangle my soul no more with the pitiful sight of thee and thy mean appearance and afflict not mine heart with care for thee I am Charisius thine husband, whom all the nation honoureth and feareth. What must I do? I know not whither to turn. What am I to think? shall I keep silence and endure? yet who can be patient when men take his treasure? and who can endure to lose thy sweet ways? and what is there for me? (Syr. thy beauties which are ever before me) the fragrance of thee is in my nostrils, and thy bright face is fixed in mine eyes. They are taking away my soul, and the fair body which I rejoiced to see they are destroying, and that sharpest of eyes they are blinding and cutting off my right hand: my joy is turning to grief and my life to death, and the light of it is being dyed (?) with darkness. Let no man of you my kindred henceforth look on me; from you no help hath come to me, nor will I hereafter worship the gods

of the east that have enwrapped me in such calamities, nor pray to them any more nor sacrifice to them, for I am bereaved of my spouse. And what else should I ask of them? for all my glory is taken away, yet am I a prince and next unto the king in power; but Mygdonia hath set me at nought, and taken away all these things. (Would that some one would blind one of my eyes, and that thine eyes would look upon me as they were wont, Syr. which has more clauses, to the same effect.)

116 And while Charisius spake thus with tears, Mygdonia sat silent and looking upon the ground; and again he came unto her and said: My lady Mygdonia, most desired of me, remember that out of all the women that are in India I chose and took thee as the most beautiful, though I might have joined to myself in marriage many more beautiful: but yet I lie, Mygdonia, for by the gods it would not have been possible to find another like thee in the land of India; but woe is me always, for thou wilt not even answer me a word: but if thou wilt, revile me, so that I may only be vouchsafed a word from thee. Look at me, for I am more comely than that sorcerer: but thou art my wealth and honour: and all men know that there is none like me: and thou art my race and kindred; and lo, he taketh thee away from me.

117 And when Charisius had so said, Mygdonia saith unto him: He whom I love is better than thee and thy substance: for thy substance is of earth and returneth unto the earth; but he whom I love is of heaven and will take me with him unto heaven. Thy wealth shall pass away, and thy beauty shall vanish, and thy robes, and thy many works: and thou shalt be alone, naked, with thy transgressions. Call not to my remembrance thy deeds (unto me), for I pray the Lord that I may forget thee, so as to remember no more those former pleasures and the custom of the body; which shall pass away as a shadow, but Jesus only endureth for ever, and the souls which hope in him. Jesus himself shall quit me of the shameful deeds which I did with thee. And when Charisius heard this, he turned him to sleep, vexed (dissolved) in soul, saying to her: Consider it by thyself all this night: and if thou wilt be with me such as thou wast before, and not see that sorcerer, I will do all according to thy mind, and if thou wilt remove thine affection from him I will take him out of the prison and let him go and remove into another country, and I will not vex thee, for I know that thou makest much of the stranger. And not with thee first did this matter come about, for many other women also hath he deceived with thee; and they have awaked sober and returned to themselves: do not thou

then make nought of my words and cause me to be a reproach among the Indians.

118 And Charisius having thus spoken went to sleep: but she took ten denarii (20 zuze, Syr.), and went secretly to give them to the gaolers that she might enter in to the apostle. But on the way Judus Thomas came and met her, and she saw him and was afraid, for she thought that he was one of the rulers: for a great light went before him. And she said to herself as she fled: have lost thee, O my unhappy soul! for thou wilt not again see Judas the apostle of [JESUS] the living [GOD], and not yet hast thou received the holy seal. And she fled and ran into a narrow place and there hid herself, saying: I would rather choose to be killed (taken) by the poorer, whom it is possible to persuade, than to fall into the hand of this mighty ruler, who will despise gifts.

THE TENTH ACT

Wherein Mygdonia receiveth baptism

119 And while Mygdonia thought thus with herself, Judas came and stood over her, and she saw him and was afraid, and fell down and became lifeless with terror. But he stood by her and took her by the hand and said unto her: Fear not, Mygdonia: Jesus will not leave thee, neither will the Lord unto whom thou hast committed thy soul overlook thee. His compassionate rest will not forsake thee: he that is kind will not forsake thee, for his kindness' sake, nor he that is good for his goodness' sake. Rise up then from the earth, thou that art become wholly above it: look on the light, for the Lord leaveth not them that love him to walk in darkness: behold him that travelleth with his servants, that he is unto them a defender in perils. And Mygdonia arose and looked on him and said: Whither wentest thou, my lord? and who is he that brought thee out of prison to behold the sun? Judas Thomas saith unto her: My Lord Jesus is mightier than all powers and all kings and rulers.

120 And Mygdonia said: Give me the seal of Jesus Christ and I shall (Let me) receive the gift at thy hands before thou departest out of life. And she took him with her and entered into the court and awaked her

nurse, saying unto her: Narcia (Gr. Marcia), my mother and nurse, all thy service and refreshment thou hast done for me from my childhood until my present age are vain, and for them I owe thee thanks which are temporal; do for me now also a favor, that thou mayest for ever receive a recompense from him that giveth great gifts. And Narcia in answer saith: What wilt thou, my daughter Mygdonia, and what is to be done for thy pleasure? for the honours which thou didst promise me before, the stranger hath not suffered thee to accomplish, and thou hast made me a reproach among all the nation. And now what is this new thing that thou commandest me? And Mygdonia saith: Become thou partaker with me in eternal life, that I may receive of thee perfect nurture: take bread and bring it me, and wine mingled with water, and spare my freedom (take pity on me a free-born woman, Syr.). And the nurse said: I will bring thee many loaves, and for water flagons of wine, and fulfil thy desire. But she saith to the nurse: Flagons I desire not, nor the many loaves: but this only, bring wine mingled with water and one loaf, and oil [EVEN be a it Syr. lamp, in if].

121 And when Narcia had brought these things, Mygdonia stood before the apostle with her head bare; and he took the oil and poured it on her head, saying: Thou holy oil given unto us for sanctification, secret mystery whereby the cross was shown unto us, thou art the straightener of the crooked limbs, thou art the humbler (softener) of hard things (works), thou art it that showeth the hidden treasures, thou art the sprout of goodness; let thy power come, let it be established upon thy servant Mygdonia, and heal thou her by this freedom. And when the oil was poured upon her he bade her nurse unclothe her and gird a linen cloth about her; and there was there a fountain of water upon which the apostle went up, and baptized Mygdonia in the name of the Father and the Son and the Holy Ghost. And when she was baptized and clad, he brake bread and took a cup of water and made her a partaker in the body of Christ and the cup of the Son of God, and said: Thou hast received thy seal, get for thyself eternal life. And immediately there was heard from above a voice saying: Yea, amen. And when Narcia heard that voice, she was amazed, and besought the apostle that she also might receive the seal; and the apostle gave it her and said: Let the care of the Lord be about thee as about the rest.

122 And having done these things the apostle returned unto the prison, and found the doors open and the guards still sleeping. And Thomas said: Who is like thee, O God? who withholdest not thy loving affection and care

from any who is like thee, the merciful, who hast delivered thy creatures out of evil. Life that hath subdued death, rest that hath ended toil. Glory be to the only-begotten of the Father. Glory to the compassionate that was sent forth of his heart. And when he had said thus, the guards waked and beheld all the doors open, and the prisoners <+ asleep, Syr.>, and said in themselves: Did not we fasten the doors? and how are they now open, and the prisoners within?

123 But at the dawn Charisius went unto Mygdonia [AND Syr. nurse, her], and found them praying and saying: O new God that by the stranger hast come hither unto us, hidden God of the dwellers in India (Syr. who art hidden from); God that hast shown thy glory by thine apostle Thomas, God whose report we have heard and believed on thee; God, unto whom we are come to be saved; God, who for love of man and for pity didst come down unto our littleness; God who didst seek us out when we knew him (thee) not; God that dwellest in the heights and from whom the depths are not hid: turn thou away from us the madness of Charisius. And Charisius hearing that said to Mygdonia: Rightly callest thou me evil and mad and foul I for if I had not borne with thy disobedience, and given thee liberty, thou wouldest not have called on God against me and made mention of my name before God. But believe me, Mygdonia that in that sorcerer there is no profit, and what he promiseth to perform he cannot: but I will perform before thy sight all that I promise, that thou mayest believe, and bear with my words and be to me as thou wast beforetime.

124 And he came near and besought her again, saying: If thou wilt be persuaded of me, I shall henceforth have no grief; remember that day when thou didst meet me first; tell the truth: was I more beautiful unto thee at that time, or Jesus at this? And Mygdonia said: That time required its own, and this time also; that was the time of the beginning, but this of the end; that was the time of temporal life, this of eternal; that of pleasure that passeth away, but this of pleasure that abideth for ever; that, of day and night, this of day without night. Thou sawest that marriage that was passing, and here, and single but this marriage continueth for ever; that was a partnership of corruption, but this of eternal life; those groomsmen (and maids) were men and women of time, but these abide unto the end. That marriage upon earth setteth up dropping dew of the love of men (Syr. That union was founded upon the earth where there is an unceasing press: this is founded upon the bridge of fire upon which is sprinkled grace: both corrupt); that bride-chamber is taken down again, but this remaineth

always; that bed was strown with coverlets (that grow old), but this with love and faith. Thou art a bridegroom that passest away and art dissolved (changed), but Jesus is a true bridegroom, enduring for ever immortal, that dowry was of money and robes that grow old, but this is of living words which never pass away.

125 And when Charisius heard these things he went unto the king and told him all: and the king commanded Judas to be brought, that he might judge him and destroy him. But Charisius said: Have patience a little, O king, and first persuade the man making him afraid, that he may persuade Mygdonia to be unto me as formerly. And Misdaeus sent and fetched the apostle of Christ, and all the prisoners were grieved because the apostle departed from them, for they yearned after him, saying: Even the comfort which we had have they taken away from us.

126 And Misdaeus said unto Judas: Wherefore teachest thou this new doctrine, which both gods and men hate, and which hath nought of profit? And Judas said: What evil do I teach? And Misdaeus said: Thou teachest, saying that men [CANNOT chastely live they except well] with the God whom thou preachest. Judas saith: Thou sayest true, O king: thus do I teach. For tell me, art thou not wroth with thy soldiers if they wait on thee in filthy garments? if then thou, being a king of earth and returning unto earth, request thy subjects to be reverend in their doings, are ye wroth and said ye that I teach ill when I say that they who serve my king must be reverend and pure and free from all grief and care of children and unprofitable riches and vain trouble? For indeed thou wouldest have thy subjects follow thy conversation and thy manners, and thou punishest them if they despise thy commandments: how much more must they that believe on him serve my God with much reverence and cleanness and security, and be quit of all pleasures of the body, adultery and prodigality and theft and drunkenness and belly-service and foul deeds?

127 And Misdaeus hearing these things said: Lo, I let thee go: go then and persuade Mygdonia, the wife of Charisius, not to desire to depart from him. Judas saith unto him: Delay not if thou hast aught to do: for her, if she hath rightly received what she hath learned, neither iron nor fire nor aught else stronger than these will avail to hurt or to root out him that is held in her soul. Misdaeus saith unto Judas: Some poisons do dissolve other poisons, and a theriac cureth the bites of the viper; and thou if thou wilt canst give a solvent of those diseases, and make peace and concord betwixt this couple: for by so doing thou wilt spare thyself, for not yet art

thou sated with life; and know thou that if thou do not persuade her, I will catch thee away out of this life which is desirable unto all men. And Judas said: This life hath been given as a loan, and this time is one that changeth, but that life whereof I teach is incorruptible; and beauty and youth that are seen shall in a little cease to be. The king saith to him: I have counselled thee for the best, but thou knowest thine own affairs.

128 And as the apostle went forth from before the king, Charisius came to him and entreated him and said: I beseech thee, O man: I have not sinned against thee or any other at any time, nor against the gods; wherefore hast thou stirred up this great calamity against me? and for what cause hast thou brought such disturbance upon mine house? and what profit hast thou of it? but if thou thinkest to gain somewhat, tell me the gain, what it is, and I will procure it for thee without labour. To what end dost thou make me mad, and cast thyself into destruction? for if thou persuade her not, I will both dispatch thee and finally take myself out of life. But if, as thou sayest, after our departing hence there is there life and death, and also condemnation and victory and a place of judgement, then will I also go in thither to be judged with thee: and if that God whom thou preachest is just and awardeth punishment justly, I know that I shall gain my cause against thee; for thou hast injured me, having suffered no wrong at my hands: for indeed even here I am able to avenge myself on thee and bring upon thee all that thou hast done unto me. Therefore be thou persuaded, and come home with me and persuade Mygdonia to be with me as she was at first, before she beheld thee. And Judas saith to him: Believe me, my child that if men loved God as much as they love one another, they would ask of him all things and receive them, and none would do them violence (there would be nothing which would not obey them, Syr.).

129 And as Thomas said this, they came unto the house of Charisius and found Mygdonia sitting and Narcia standing by her, and her hand supporting her cheek; and she was saying: Let the remainder of the days of my life, O mother, be cut off from me, and all the hours become as one hour, and let me depart out of life that I may go the sooner and behold that beautiful one, whose report I have heard, even that living one and giver of life unto them that believe on him, where is not day and night, nor light and darkness, nor good and evil, nor poor and rich, nor male and female, nor free and bond, nor proud that subjecteth the humble. And as she spake the apostle stood by her, and forthwith she rose up and did him reverence. Then Charisius said unto him: Seest thou how she feareth and honoureth

thee and all that thou shalt bid her she will do willingly?

130 And as he so spake, Judas saith unto Mygdonia: My daughter Mygdonia, obey that which thy brother Charisius saith. And Mygdonia saith: If thou wast not able [TO name] the deed in word wilt thou compel me to endure the act? for I have heard of thee that this life is of no profit, and this relief is for a time, and these possessions are transitory. And again thou saidst that whoso renounceth this life shall receive the life eternal, and whoso hateth the light of day and night shall behold a light that is not overtaken, that whoso despiseth this money shall find other and eternal money. But now [THOU things these sayest] because thou art in fear. Who that hath done somewhat and is praised for the work changeth it? [WHO and a tower buildeth] straightway overthroweth it from the foundation? who diggeth a spring water in a thirsty land and straightway filleth it in? who findeth a treasure and useth it not? And Charisius heard lt. and said: I will not imitate you, neither will I hasten to destroy you; nor though I may so do, will I put bonds about thee (but thee I will bind, Syr.); and I will not suffer thee to speak with this sorcerer; and if thou obey me, well, but if not, I know what I must do.

131 And Judas went out of Charisius' house and departed unto the house of Siphor and lodged there with him. And Siphor said: I will prepare for Judas a hall (triclinium) wherein he may teach (Syr. Siphor said to Judas: Prepare thyself an apartment, &c.). And he did so; and Siphor said : I and my wife and daughter will dwell henceforth in holiness, and in chastity, and in one affection. I beseech thee that we may receive of thee the seal, and become worshippers of the true God and numbered among his sheep and lambs. And Judas said: I am afraid to speak that which I think: yet I know somewhat, and what I know it is not possible for me to utter.

132 And he began to say concerning baptism: This baptism is remission of sins (the Greek MSS. U and P have divergent texts, both obscure): this bringeth forth again light that is shed about us: this bringeth to new birth the new man (this is the restorer of understandings Syr.): this mingleth the spirit (with the body), raiseth up in threefoldwise a new man and [MAKETH him] partaker of the remission of sins. Glory be to thee, hidden one, that art communicated in baptism. Glory to thee the unseen power that is in baptism. Glory to thee, renewal, whereby are renewed they that are baptized and with affection take hold upon thee.

And having thus said, he poured oil over their heads and said: Glory be to thee the love of compassion (bowels). Glory to thee name of Christ.

Glory to thee, power established in Christ. And he commanded a vessel to be brought, and baptized them in the name of the Father and the Son and the Holy Ghost.

133 And when they were baptized and clad, he set bread on the table and blessed it, and said: Bread of life, the which who eat abide incorruptible: Bread that filleth the hungry souls with the blessing thereof: thou art he that vouchsafest to receive a gift, that thou mayest become unto us remission of sins, and that they who eat thee may become immortal: we invoke upon thee the name of the mother, of the unspeakable mystery of the hidden powers and authorities (? we name the name of the unspeakable mystery, that is hidden from all &c.): we invoke upon thee the name of [thy?] Jesus. And he said: Let the powers of blessing come, and be established in this bread, that all the souls which partake of it may be washed from their sins. And he brake and gave unto Siphor and his wife and daughter.

THE ELEVENTH ACT

Concerning the wife of Misdaeus

134 Now Misdaeus the king, when he had let Judas go, dined and went home, and told his wife what had befallen Charisius their kinsman, saying: See what hath come to pass to that unhappy man, and thou thyself knowest, my sister Tertia, that a man hath nought better than his own wife on whom he resteth; but it chanced that his wife went unto that sorcerer of whom thou hast heard that he is come to the land of the Indians, and fell into his charms and is parted from her own husband; and he knoweth not what he should do. And when I would have destroyed the malefactor, he would not have it. But do thou go and counsel her to incline unto her husband, and forsake the vain words of the sorcerer.

135 And as soon as she arose Tertia went to the house of Charisius her husband's [KINSMAN], and found Mygdonia Lying upon the earth in humiliation, and ashes and sackcloth were spread under her, and she was praying that the Lord would forgive her her former sins and she might soon depart out of life. And Tertia said unto her: Mygdonia, my dear sister and companion what is this hand (Syr. this folly)? what is the disease that hath

overtaken thee? and why doest thou the deeds of madmen? Know thyself and come back unto thine own way, come near unto thy many kinsfolk, and spare thy true husband Charisius, and do not things unbefitting a free-woman. Mygdonia saith unto her: O Tertia, thou hast not yet heard the preacher of life: not yet hath he touched thine ears, not yet hast thou tasted the medicine of life nor art freed from corruptible mourning. Thou standest in the life of time, and the everlasting life and salvation thou knowest not, and perceivest not the incorruptible fellowship. Thou standest clad in robes that grow old and desirest not those that are eternal, and art proud of this beauty which vanisheth and hast no thought of the holiness of thy soul; and art rich in a multitude of servants, (and hast not freed thine own soul from servitude, Syr.) and pridest thyself in the glory that cometh of many, but redeemest not thyself from the condemnation of death.

136 And when Tertia heard this of Mygdonia she said: I pray thee, sister, bring me unto that stranger that teacheth these great things, that I also may go and hear him, and be taught to worship the God whom he preacheth, and become partaker of his prayers, and a sharer in all that thou hast told me of. And Mygdonia saith to her: He is in the house of Siphor the captain; for he is become the occasion of life unto all them that are being saved in India. And hearing that, Tertia went quickly to Siphor's house, that she might see the new apostle that was come thither. And when she entered in, Judas said unto her: What art thou come to see? a man that is a stranger and poor and contemptible and needy, having neither riches nor substance; yet one thing I possess which neither kings nor rulers can take away, that neither perisheth nor ceaseth, which is Jesus the Saviour of all mankind, the Son of the living God, who hath given life unto all that believe on him and take refuge with him and are known to be of the number of his servants (sheep, Syr.). Unto whom saith Tertia: May I become a partaker of this life which thou promisest that all they shall receive who come together unto the assembly of God. And the apostle said: The treasury of the holy king is opened wide, and they which worthily partake of the good things that are therein do rest, and resting do reign: but first, no man cometh unto him that is unclean and vile: for he knoweth our inmost hearts and the depths of our thought, and it is not possible for any to escape him. Thou, then, if verily thou believest in him, shalt be made worthy of his mysteries; and he will magnify thee and enrich thee, and make thee to be an heir of his hingdom.

137 And Tertia having heard this returned home rejoicing, and found

her husband awaiting her, not having dined, and when Misdaeus saw her he said: Whence is it that thine entering in to-day is more beautiful? and wherefore art thou come walking, which beseemeth not free-born women like thee? And Tertia saith unto him: I owe thee the greatest of thanks for that thou didst send me unto Mygdonia, for I went and heard of a new life, and I saw the new apostle of the God that giveth life unto them that believe on him and fulfil his commandments; I ought therefore myself to recompense thee for this favour and admonition with good advice; for thou shalt be a great king in heaven if thou obey me and fear the God that is preached by the strangrer, and keep thyself holy unto the living God. For this kingdom passeth away, and thy comfort will be turned into affliction: but go thou to that man, and believe him, and thou shalt live unto the end. And when Misdaeus heard these things of his wife, he smote his face with his hands and rent his clothes and said: May the soul of Charisius find no rest, for he hath hurt me to the soul; and may he have no hope, for he hath taken away my hope. And he went out greatly vexed.

138 And he found Charisius his friend in the market-place, and said unto him: Why hast thou cast me into hell to be another companion to thyself? why hast thou emptied and defrauded me to gain nought? why hast thou hurt me and profited thyself not at all? why hast thou slain me and thyself not lived? Why hast thou wronged me and thyself not got justice? why didst thou not suffer me to destroy that sorcerer before he corrupted my house with his wickedness? And he kept hold upon (was upbraiding, Syr.) Charisius. And Charisius saith: Why, what hath befallen thee? Misdaeus said: He hath bewitched Tertia. And they went both of them unto the house of Siphor the captain, and found Judas sitting and teaching. And all they that were there rose up before the king, but he arose not. And Misdaeus perceived that it was he, and took hold of the seat and overset it, and took up the seat with both his hands and smote his head so that he wounded it, and delivered him to his soldiers, saying: Take him away, and hale him with violence and not gently, that his shame may be manifest unto all men. And they haled him and took him to the place where Misdaeus judged, and he stood there, held of the soldiers of Misdaeus.

THE TWELFTH ACT

Concerning Ouazanes (Iuzanes) the son of Misdaeus

139 And Ouazanes (Iuzanes, P; Vizan, Syr.) the son of Misdaeus came unto the soldiers and said: Give me him that I may speak with him until the king cometh. And they gave him up, and he brought him in where the king gave judgement. And Iuzanes saith: Knowest thou not that I am the son of Misdaeus the king, and I have power to say unto the king what I will, and he will suffer thee to live? tell me then, who is thy God, and what power dost thou claim and glory in it? for if it be some power or art of magic, tell it me and teach me, and I will let thee go. Judas saith unto him: Thou art the son of Misdacus the king who is king for a time, but I am the servant of Jesus Christ the eternal king, and thou hast power to say to thy father to save whom thou wilt in the temporal life wherein men continue not, which thou and thy father grant, but I beseech my Lord and intercede for men, and he giveth them a new life which is altogether enduring. And thou boastest thyself of possessions and servants and robes and luxury and unclean chamberings, but I boast myself of poverty and philosophy and humility and lasting and prayer and the fellowship of the Holy Ghost and of my brethren that are worthy of God: and I boast myself of eternal life. And thou reliest on (hast taken refuge with) a man like unto thyself and not able to save his own soul from judgement and death, but I rely upon the living God, upon the saviour of kings and princes, who is the judge of all men. And ye indeed to-day perchance are, and to-morrow are no more, but I have taken refuge with him that abideth for ever and knoweth all our seasons and times. And if thou wilt become the servant of this God thou shalt soon do so; but show that thou wilt be a servant worthy of him hereby: first by holiness (purity), which is the head of all good things, and then by fellowship with this God whom I preach, and philosophy and simplicity and love and faith and [GOOD hope] in him, and unity of pure food (simplicity of pure i e, Syr.).

140   And the young man was persuaded by the Lord and sought occasion how he might let Judas escape: but while he thought thereon, the king came, and the soldiers took Judas and led him forth. And Iuzanes went forth with him and stood beside him. And when the king was set he bade Judas be brought in, with his hands bound behind him; and he was brought into the midst and stood there. And the king saith: Tell me who

thou art and by what power thou doest these things. And Judas saith to him: I am a man like thee, and by the power of Jesus Christ I do these things. And Misdaeus saith: Tell me the truth before I destroy thee. And Judas saith: Thou hast no power against me, as thou supposest, and thou wilt not hurt me at all. And the king was wroth at his words, and commanded to heat iron plates and set him upon them barefoot; and as the soldiers took off his shoes he said: The wisdom of God is better than the wisdom of men. Thou Lord and King (do thou take counsel against them, Syr.) and let thy goodness resist his wrath. And they brought the plates which were like fire, and set the apostle upon them, and straightway water sprang up abundantly from the earth, so that the plates were swallowed up in it, and they that held him let him go and withdrew themselves.

141 And the king seeing the abundance of water said to Judas: Ask thy God that he deliver me from this death, that I perish not in the flood. And the apostle prayed and said: Thou that didst bind this element (nature) and gather it into one place and send it forth into divers lands; that didst bring disorder into order, that grantest mighty works and great wonders by the hands of Judas thy servant; that hast mercy on my soul, that I may always receive thy brightness; that givest wages unto them that have laboured; thou saviour of my soul, restoring it unto its own nature that it may have no fellowship with hurtful things; that hast always been the occasion of life: do thou restrain this element that it lift not up itself to destroy; for there are some of them that stand here who shall believe on thee and live. And when he had prayed, the water was swallowed up by little and little, and the place became dry. And when Misdaeus saw it he commanded him to be taken to the prison: Until I shall consider how he must be used.

142 And as Judas was led away to the prison they all followed him, and Iuzanes the king's son walked at his right hand, and Siphor at the left. And he entered into the prison and sat down, and Iuzanes and Siphor, and he persuaded his wife and his daughter to sit down, for they also were come in to hear the word of life. For they knew that Misdaeus would slay him because of the excess of his anger. And Judas began to say: O liberator of my soul from the bondage of the many, because I gave myself to be sold [UNTO Syr. one,]; behold, I rejoice and exult, knowing that the times are fulfilled for me to enter in and receive [THEE of my Syr. rest, giver]. Lo, I am to be set free from the cares that are on the earth; lo, I fulfil mine hope and receive truth; lo, I am set free from sorrow and put on joy alone; lo, I become careless and griefless and dwell in rest; lo, I am set free from

bondage and am called unto liberty; lo, I have served times and seasons, and I am lifted up above times and seasons; lo, I receive my wages from my recompenser, who giveth without reckoning (number) because his wealth sufficeth for the gift; [LO, and my raiment, on off put I] and I shall not put it on again; lo, I sleep and awake, and I shall no more go to sleep; lo, I die and live again, and I shall no more taste of death; lo, they rejoice and expect me, that I may come and be with their kindred and be set as a flower in their crown; lo, I reign in the kingdom whereon I set my hope, even from hence; lo, the rebellious fall before me, for I have escaped them; lo, (unto me) the peace hath come, whereunto all are gathered.

143 And as the apostle spake thus, all that were there hearkened, supposing that in that hour he would depart out of life. And again he said: Believe on the physician of all [DISEASES], both seen and unseen, and on the saviour of the souls that need help from him. This is the free-born [SON] of kings, this the physician of his creatures; this is he that was reproached of his own slaves; this is the Father of the height and the Lord of nature and the Judge (? Father of nature and Lord of the height and supreme Judge, Syr.): he came of the greatest, the only-begotten son of the deep; and he was called the son of (became visible through, Syr.) Mary the virgin, and was termed the son of Joseph the carpenter: he whose littleness (we beheld) with the eyes of our body, but his greatness we received by faith, and saw it in his works whose human body we felt also with our hands, and his aspect we saw transfigured (changed) with our eyes, but his heavenly semblance on the mount we were not able to see: he that made the rulers stumble and did violence unto death: he, the truth that lieth not, that at the last paid the tribute for himself and his disciples: whom the prince beholding feared and the powers that were with him were troubled; and the prince bare witness (asked him, Syr.) who he was and from whence, and knew not the truth, because he is alien from truth: he that having authority over the world, and the pleasures therein, and the possessions and the comfort, [REJECTED] all these things and turneth away his subjects, that they should not use them.

144 And having fulfilled these sayings, he arose and prayed thus: our Father, which art in heaven: hallowed be thy name: Thy kingdom come: Thy will be done, as in heaven so upon earth: [GIVE the of Syr. day, bread constant us] and forgive us our debts as we also have forgiven our debtors. And lead us not into temptation, but deliver us from the evil one.

My Lord and God, hope and confidence and teacher, thou hast taught me to pray thus, behold, I pray this prayer and fulfil thy commandment: be thou with me unto the end; thou art he that from childhood hast sown life in me and kept me from corruption; thou art he that hast brought me unto the poverty of this world, and exhorted me unto the true riches; thou art he that hast made me known unto myself and showed me that I am thine; and I have kept myself pure from woman, that that which thou requirest be not found in defilement.

[At the words 'My Lord and God' begins the double text, represented on the one hand by the MS. U and on the other by the Paris MS. P, and three (partly four) others. These insert the prayer after ch. 167. Their text, I believe, may be the original Greek. I follow it here, repeating the first paragraph.]

(144) My Lord and God, my hope and my confidence and my teacher, that hast implanted courage in me, thou didst teach me to pray thus; behold, I pray thy prayer and bring thy will to fulfilment: be thou with me unto the end. Thou art he that from my youth up didst give me patience in temptation and [SOW in] me life and preserve me from corruption; thou art he that didst bring me into the poverty of this world and fill me with the true riches; thou art he that didst show me that I was thine: wherefore I was never joined unto a wife, that the temple worthy of thee might not be found in pollution.

145 My mouth sufficeth not to praise thee, neither am I able to conceive the care and providence (carefulness) which hath been about me from thee which thou hast had for me). For I desired to gain riches, but thou by a vision didst show me that they are full of loss and injury to them that gain them and I believed thy showing, and continued in the poverty of the world until thou, the true riches wert revealed unto me, who didst fill both me and the rest that were worthy of thee with thine own riches and set free thine own from care and anxiety. I have therefore fulfilled thy commandments, O Lord, and accomplished thy will, and become poor and needy and a stranger and a bondman and set at nought and a prisoner and hungry and thirsty and naked and unshod, and I have toiled for thy sake, that my confidence might not perish and my hope that is in thee might not be confounded and my much labour might not be in vain and my weariness not be counted for nought: let not my prayers and my continual fastings perish, and my great zeal toward thee; let not my seed of wheat be changed for tares out of thy land, Let not the enemy carry it away and mingle his own tares therewith; for thy land verily receiveth not his tares, neither indeed can they be laid up in thine houses.

146 I have planted thy vine in the earth, it hath sent down its roots into the depth and its growth is spread out in the height, and the fruits of it are stretched forth upon the earth, and they that are worthy of thee are made glad by them, whom also thou hast gained. The money which thou hast from me I laid down upon the table (bank); this, when thou requirest it, restore unto me with usury, as thou hast promised. With thy one mind have I traded and have made ten, thou hast added more to me beside that I had, as thou didst covenant. I have forgiven my debtor the mine, require thou it not at my hands. I was bidden to the supper and I came: and I refused the land and the yoke of oxen and the wife, that I might not for their sake be rejected; I was bidden to the wedding, and I put on white raiment, that I might be worthy of it and not be bound hand and foot and cast into the outer darkness. My lamp with its bright light expecteth the master coming from the marriage, that it may receive him, and I may not (? he may not) see it dimmed because the oil is spent. Mine eyes, O Christ, look upon thee, and mine heart exulteth with joy because I have fulfilled thy will and perfected thy commandments; that I may be likened unto that watchful and careful servant who in his eagerness neglecteth not to keep vigil (other MSS.: I have not slumbered idly in keeping thy commandments: in the first sleep and at midnight and at cockcrow, that mine eyes may behold thee, &c.). All the night have I laboured to keep mine house from robbers, lest it be broken through.

147 My loins have I girt close with truth and bound my shoes on my feet, that I may never see them gaping: mine hands have I put unto the yoked plough and have not turned away backward, lest my furrows go crooked. The plough-land is become white and the harvest is come, that I may receive my wages. My garment that groweth old I have worn out, and the labour that hath brought me unto rest have I accomplished. I have kept the first watch and the second and the third, that I may behold thy face and adore thine holy brightness. I have rooted out the worst (pulled down my barns, Syr.) and left them desolate upon earth, that I may be filled full from thy treasures (Gr. MSS. add: all my substance have I sold, that I may gain thee the pearl). The moist spring that was in me have I dried up, that I may live and rest beside thine inexhaustible spring (al. and Syr.: rest beside thy living spring). The captive whom thou didst commit to me I have slain, that he which is set free in me may not fall from his confidence. Him that was inward have I made outward and the outward [INWARD], and all thy fullness hath been fulfilled in me. I have not returned unto the things

that are behind, but have gone forward unto the things that are before, that I become not a reproach. The dead man have I quickened, and the living one have I overcome, and that which was lacking have I filled up (Syr. Wright, not the older one, inserts negatives, ' not quickened ', &c.), that I may receive the crown of victory, and the power of Christ may be accomplished in me. I have received reproach upon earth, but give thou me the return and the recompense in the heavens. (U omits practically all this chapter.)

148 Let not the powers and the officers perceive me, and let them not have any thought concerning me; let not the publicans and exactors ply their calling upon me; let not the weak and the evil cry out against me that am valiant and humble, and when I am borne upward let them not rise up to stand before me, by thy power, O Jesu, which surroundeth me as a crown: for they do flee and hide themselves, they cannot look on thee: but (for) suddenly do they fall upon them that are subject to them, and the portion of tile sons of the evil one doth itself cry out and convict them; and it is not hid from them, nor their nature is made known: the children of the evil one are separated off. Do thou then grant me, Lord, that I may pass by in quietness and joy and peace, and pass over and stand before the judge, and let not the devil (or slanderer) look upon me; let his eyes be blinded by thy light which thou hast made to dwell in me, close thou up (muzzle) his mouth: for he hath found nought against me.

[We revert to U.]

149 And he said again unto them that were about him: believe in the Saviour of them that have laboured in his service: for my soul already flourisheth because my time is near to receive him; for he being beautiful draweth me on always to speak concerning his beauty, what it is though I be not able and suffice not to speak it worthily: thou that art the light (feeder, Syr.) of my poverty and the supplier of my defects and nurturer of my need: be thou with me until I come and receive thee for evermore.

THE THIRTEENTH ACT

Wherein Iuzanes receiveth baptism with the rest

150 And Iuzanes the youth besought the apostle, saying: I pray thee,
O man, apostle of God, suffer me to go, and I will persuade the gaoler
to permit thee to come home with me, that by thee I may receive the
seal, and become thy minister and a keeper of the commandments of the
God whom thou preachest. For indeed, formerly I walked in those things
which thou teachest, until my father compelled me and joined me unto a
wife by name Mnesara; for I am in my one-and-twentieth year, and have
now been seven years married, and before I was joined in marriage I knew
no other woman, wherefore also I was accounted useless of my father,
nor have I ever had son or daughter of this wife and also my wife herself
hath lived with me in chastity all this time, and to-day, if she had been in
health, and had listened to thee, I know well that both I should have been
at rest and she would have received eternal life; but she is in peril and
afflicted with much illness; I will therefore persuade the keeper that he
promise to come with me, for I live by myself: and thou shalt also heal
that unhappy one. And Judas the apostle of the Most High, hearing this,
said to Iuzanes: If thou believest, thou shalt see the marvels of God, and
how he sayeth his servants.

151 And as they spake thus together, Tertia and Mvgdonia and Narcia
stood at the door of the prison, and they gave the gaoler 363 staters of
silver and entered in to Judas; and found Iuzanes and Siphor and his wife
and daughter, and all the prisoners sitting and hearing the word. And when
they stood by him he said to them: Who hath suffered you to come unto
us? and who opened unto you the sealed door that ye came forth? Tertia
saith unto him: Didst not thou open the door for us and tell us to come into
the prison that we might take our brethren that were there, and then should
the Lord show forth his glory in us? And when we came near the door, I
know not how, thou wast parted from us and hid thyself and camest hither
before us where also we heard the noise of the door, when thou didst shut
us out. We gave money therefore to the keepers and came in and lo, we
are here praying thee that we may persuade thee and let thee escape until
the king's wrath against thee shall cease. Unto whom Judas said: Tell us
first of all how ye were shut up.

152 And she saith to him: Thou wast with us, and didst never leave us
for one hour, and askest thou how we were shut up? but if thou desirest

to hear, hear. The king Misdaeus sent for me and said unto me: Not yet hath that sorcerer prevailed over thee, for, as I hear, he bewitcheth men with oil and water and bread, and hath not yet bewitched thee; but obey thou me, for if not, I will imprison thee and wear thee out, and him I will destroy; for I know that if he hath not yet given thee oil and water and bread, he hath not prevailed to get power over thee. And I said unto him: Over my body thou hast authority, and do thou all that thou wilt; but my soul I will not let perish with thee. And hearing that he shut me up in a chamber (beneath his dining-hall, Syr.): and Charisius brought Mygdonia and shut her up with me: and thou broughtest us out and didst bring us even hither; but give thou us the seal quickly, that the hope of Misdacus who counselleth thus may be cut off.

153 And when the apostle heard this, he said: Glory be to thee, O Jesu of many forms, glory to thee that appearest in the guise of our poor manhood: glory to thee that encouragest us and makest us strong and givest grace and consolest and standest by us in all perils, and strengthenest our weakness. And as he thus spake, the gaoler came and said: Put out the lamps, lest any accuse you unto the king. And then they extinguished the lamps, and turned to sleep; but the apostle spake unto the Lord: It is the time now, O Jesu, for thee to make haste; for, lo the children of darkness sit (make us to sit, Syr.) in their own darkness, do thou therefore enlighten us with the light of thy nature. And on a sudden the whole prison was light as the day: and while all they that were in the prison slept a deep sleep, they only that had believed in the Lord continued waking.

154 Judas therefore saith to Iuzanes: Go thou before and make ready the things for our need. Iuzanes therefore saith: And who will open me the doors of the prison? for the gaolers shut them and are gone to sleep. And Judas saith: Believe in Jesus, and thou shalt find the doors open. And when he went forth and departed from them, all the rest followed after him. And as Iuzanes was gone on before, Mnesara his wife met him coming unto the prison. And she knew him and said: My brother Iuzanes, is it thou? and he saith, Yea, and art thou Mnesara? and she saith Yea. Iuzanes said unto her; Whither walkest thou, especially at so untimely an hour? and how wast thou able to rise up? And she said: This youth laid his hand on me and raised me up, and in a dream I say that I should go where the stranger sitteth, and become perfectly whole. Iuzanes saith to her: What youth is with thee? And she said: Seest thou not him that is on my right hand, leading me by the hand?

155 And while they spake together thus, Judas, with Siphor and his wife and daughter and Tertia and Mygdonia and Narcia came unto Iuzanes' house. And Mnesara the wife of Iuzanes seeing him did reverence and said: Art thou come that sayedst us from the sore disease? thou art he whom I saw in the night delivering unto me this youth to bring me to the prison. But thy goodness suffered me not to grow weary, but thou thyself art come unto me. And so saying she turned about and saw the youth no more; and finding him not, she saith to the apostle: I am not able to walk alone: for the youth whom thou gavest me is not here. And Judas said: Jesus will henceforth lead thee. And thereafter she came running unto him. And when they entered into the house of Iuzanes the son of Misdaeus the king though it was yet night, a great light shined and was shed about them.

156 And then Judas began to pray and to speak thus: O companion and defender (ally) and hope of the weak and confidence of the poor: refuge and lodging of the weary: voice that came forth of the height (sleep, Gr.): comforter dwelling in the midst: port and harbour of them that pass through the regions of the rulers: physician that healest without payment: who among men wast crucified for many: who didst go down into hell with great might: the sight of whom the princes of death endured not; and thou camest up with great glory, and gathering all them that fled unto thee didst prepare a way, and in thy footsteps all they journeyed whom thou didst redeem; and thou broughtest them into thine own fold and didst join them with thy sheep: son of mercy, the son that for love of man wast sent unto us from the perfect country (fatherland) that is above, the Lord of all possessions (undefiled possessions, Syr.): that servest thy servants that they may live: that fillest creation with thine own riches: the poor, that wast in need and didst hunger forty days: that satisfiest thirsty souls with thine own good things; be thou with Iuzanes the son of Misdaeus and with Tertia and Mnesara, and gather them into thy fold and mingle them with thy number; Be unto them a guide in the land of error: be unto them a physician in the land of sickness: be unto them a rest in the land of the weary: sanctify them in a polluted land: be their physician both of bodies and souls: make them holy temples of thee, and let thine holy spirit dwell in them.

157 Having thus prayed over them, the apostle said unto Mygdonia: Unclothe thy sisters. And she took off their clothes and girded them with girdles and brought them: but Iuzanes had first gone before, and they

came after him; and the apostle took oil in a cup of silver and spake thus over it: Fruit more beautiful than all other fruits, unto which none other whatsoever may be compared: altogether merciful: fervent with the force of the word: power of the tree which men putting upon them overcome their adversaries: crowner of the conquerors: help (symbol) and joy of the sick: that didst announce unto men their salvation that showest light to them that are in darkness; whose leaf is bitter, but in thy most sweet fruit thou art fair, that art rough to the sight but soft to the taste; seeming to be weak, but in the greatness of thy strength able to bear the power that beholdeth all things. Having thus said [a corrupt word follows]: Jesu: let his victorious might come and be established in this oil, like as it was established in the tree (wood) that was its kin, even his might at that time, whereof they that crucified thee could not endure the word: let the gift also come whereby breathing upon his (thine) enemies thou didst cause them to go backward and fall headlong and let it rest on this oil, whereupon we invoke thine holy name. And having thus said, he poured it first upon the head of Iuzanes and then upon the women's heads, saying: In thy name, O Jesu Christ, let it be unto these souls for remission of sins and for turning back of the adversary and for salvation of their souls. And he commanded Mygdonia to anoint them but he himself anointed Iuzanes. And having anointed them he led them down into the water in the name of the Father and the Son and the Holy Ghost.

158 And when they were come up, he took bread and a cup, and blessed it and said: Thine holy body w}lich was crucified for us do we eat, and thy blood that was shed for us unto salvation do we drink; let therefore thy body be unto us salvation and thy blood for remission of sins. And for the gall which thou didst drink for our sakes let the gall of the devil be removed from us: and for the vinegar which thou hast drunk for us, let our weakness be made strong: and for the spitting which thou didst receive for us, let us receive the dew of thy goodness: and by (or for) the reed wherewith they smote thee for us, let us receive the perfect house: and whereas thou receivedst a crown of thorns for our sake, let us that have loved thee put on a crown that fadeth not away; and for the linen cloth wherein thou wast Wrapped, let us also be girt about with thy power that is not vanquished and for the new tomb and the burial let us receive renewing of soul and body: and for that thou didst rise up and revive, let us revive and live and stand before thee in righteous judgement. And he brake and gave the eucharist unto Iuzanes and Tertia and Mnesara and the

wife and daughter of Siphor and said: Let this eucharist be unto you for salvation and joy and health of your souls. And they said: Amen. And a voice was heard, saying: Amen: fear ye not, but only believe.

[THE MARTYRDOM Here we revert to the text of P and its companions.]

159 And after these things Judas departed to be imprisoned.

And Tertia with Mygdonia and Narcia also went to be imprisoned. And the apostle Thomas said unto them -the multitude of them that had believed being present: Daughters and sisters and fellow-servants which have believed in my Lord and God, ministers of my Jesus, hearken to me this day: for I do deliver my word unto you, and I shall no more speak with you in this flesh nor in this world; for I go up unto my Lord and God Jesus Christ, unto him that sold me, unto that Lord that humbled himself even unto me the little, and brought me up unto eternal greatness, that vouchsafed to me to become his servant in truth and steadfastness: unto him do I depart, knowing that the time is fulfilled, and the day appointed hath drawn near for me to go and receive my recompense from my Lord and God: for my recompenser is righteous, who knoweth me, how I ought to receive my reward; for he is not grudging nor envious, but is rich in his gifts, he is not a lover of craft (OT sparing) in that he giveth, for he hath confidence in his possessions which cannot fail.

160 I am not Jesus, but I am his servant: I am not Christ, but I am his minister; I am not the Son of God, but I pray to become worthy of God. Continue ye in the faith of Christ: continue in the hope of the Son of God: faint not at affliction, neither be divided in mind if ye see me mocked or that I am shut up in prison [OR Syr. die,]; for I do accomplish his will. For if I had willed not to die, I know in Christ that I am able thereto: but this which is called death, is not death, but a setting free from the body; wherefore I receive gladly this setting free from the body, that I may depart and see him that is beautiful and full of mercy, him that is to be loved: for I have endured much toil in his service, and have laboured for his grace that is come upon me, which departeth not from me. Let not Satan, then, enter you by stealth and catch away your thoughts: let there be in you no place for him: for he is mighty whom ye have received. Look for the coming of Christ, for he shall come and receive you, and this is he whom ye shall see when he cometh.

161 When the apostle had ended these sayings, they went into the house, and the apostle Thomas said: Saviour that didst suffer many things

for us, let these doors be as they were and let seals be set on them. And he left them and went to be imprisoned: and they wept and were in heaviness, for they knew that Misdaeus would slay him (not knowing that, M. would release him, P.).

162 And the apostle found the keepers wrangling and saying: Wherein have we sinned against this wizard? for by his art magic he hath opened the doors and would have had all the prisoners escape: but let us go and report it unto the king, and tell him concerning his wife and his son. And as they disputed thus, Thomas held his peace. They rose up early, therefore, and went unto the king and said unto him: Our lord and king, do thou take away that sorcerer and cause him to be shut up elsewhere, for we are not able to keep him; for except thy good fortune had kept the prison, all the condemned persons would have escaped for now this second time have we found the doors open: and also thy wife, O king, and thy son and the rest depart not from him. And the king, hearing that, went, and found the seals that were set on the doors whole; and he took note of the doors also, and said to the keepers: Wherefore lie ye? for the seals are whole. How said ye that Tertia and Mygdonia come unto him into the prison? And the keepers said: We have told thee the truth.

163 And Misdaeus went to the prison and took his seat, and sent for the apostle Thomas and stripped him (and girded him with a girdle) and set him before him and saith unto him: Art thou bond or free? Thomas said: I am the bondsman of one only, over whom thou hast no authority. And Misdaeus saith to him: How didst thou run away and come into this country? And Thomas said: I was sold hither by my master, that I might save many, and by thy hands depart out of this world. And Misdaeus said: Who is thy lord? and what is his name? and of what country is he? And Thomas said: My Lord is thy master and he is Lord of heaven and earth. And Misdaeus saith: What is his name? Thomas saith: Thou canst not hear his true name at this time: but the name that was given unto him is Jesus Christ. And Misdaeus saith unto him: I have not made haste to destroy thee, but have had long patience with thee: but thou hast added unto thine evil deeds, and thy sorceries are dispersed abroad and heard of throughout all the country: but this I do that thy sorceries may depart with thee, and our land be cleansed from them. Thomas saith unto him; These sorceries depart [NOT, Syr.] with me when I set forth hence, and know thou this that I [THEY, Syr.] shall never forsake them that are here.

164 When the apostle had said these things, Misdaeus considered how

he should put him to death; for he was afraid because of the much people that were subject unto him, for many also of the nobles and of them that were in authority believed on him. He took him therefore and went forth out of the city; and armed soldiers also went with him. And the people supposed that the king desired to learn somewhat of him, and they stood still and gave heed. And when they had walked one mile, he delivered him unto four soldiers and an officer, and commanded them to take him into the mountain and there pierce him with spears and put an end to him, and return again to the city. And saying thus unto the soldiers, he himself also returned unto the city.

165 But the men ran after Thomas, desiring to deliver him from death. And two soldiers went at the right hand of the apostle and two on his left, holding spears, and the officer held his hand and supported him. And the apostle Thomas said: O the hidden mysteries which even until our departure are accomplished in us! O riches of his glory, who will not suffer us to be swallowed up in this passion of the body! Four are they that cast me down, for of four am I made; and one is he that draweth me, for of one I am, and unto him I go. And this I now understand, that my Lord and God Jesus Christ being of one was pierced by one, but I, which am of four, am pierced by four.

166 And being come up into the mountain unto the place where he was to be slain, he said unto them that held him, and to the rest: Brethren, hearken unto me now at the last; for I am come to my departure out of the body. Let not then the eyes of your heart be blinded, nor your ears be made deaf. Believe on the God whom I preach, and be not guides unto yourselves in the hardness of your heart, but walk in all your liberty, and in the glory that is toward men, and the life that is toward God.

167 And he said unto Iuzanes: Thou son (to the son, P) of the (earthly) king Misdaeus and minister (to the minister) of our Lord Jesus Christ: give unto the servants of Misdaeus their price that they may suffer me to go and pray. And Iuzanes persuaded the soldiers to let him pray. And the blessed Thomas went to pray, and kneeled down, and rose up and stretched forth his hands unto heaven, and spake thus:

[Here P and the rest give - rightly - the prayer of cc. 144-8. U and its companions give the following: He turned to his prayer; and it was this: My Lord and my God, and hope and redeemer and leader and guide in all countries, be thou with all them that serve thee, and guide me this day as I come unto thee. Let not any take my soul which I have committed unto thee: let not the publicans see me, and let not the exactors accuse me falsely (play the sycophant with me). Let not the serpent see me, and let not the children of the dragon hiss at me. Behold, Lord, I have accomplished thy work and perfected thy commandment. I have become a bondman; therefore to-day do I receive freedom. Do thou therefore give me this and perfect me: and this I say, not for that I doubt, but that they may hear for whom it is needful to hear.]

168 And when he had thus prayed he said unto the soldiers: Come hither and accomplish the commandments of him that sent you. And the four came and pierced him with their spears, and he fell down and died.

And all the brethren wept; and they brought beautiful robes and much and fair linen, and buried him in a royal sepulchre wherein the former (first) kings were laid.

169 But Siphor and Iuzanes would not go down to the city, but continued sitting by him all the day. And the apostle Thomas appeared unto them and said: Why sit ye here and keep watch over me? I am not here, but I have gone up and received all that I was promised. But rise up and go down hence; for after a little time ye also shall be gathered unto me.

But Misdaeus and Charisius took away Mygdonia and Tertia and afflicted them sorely: howbeit they consented not unto their will. And the apostle appeared unto them and said: Be not deceived: Jesus the holy, the living one, shall quickly send help unto you. And Misdaeus and Charisius, when they perceived that Mygdonia and Tertia obeyed them not, suffered them to live according to their own desire.

And the brethren gathered together and rejoiced in the grace of the Holy Ghost: now the apostle Thomas when he departed out of the world made Siphor a presbyter and Iuzanes a deacon, when he went up into the mountain to die. And the Lord wrought with them, and many were added unto the faith.

170 Now it came to pass after a long time that one of the children of Misdaeus the king was smitten by a devil, and no man could cure him, for the devil was exceeding fierce. And Misdaeus the king took thought and sad: I will go and open the sepulchre, and take a bone of the apostle of God and hang it upon my son and he shall be healed. But while Misdaeus thought upon this, the apostle Thomas appeared to him and said unto him: Thou believedst not on a living man, and wilt thou believe on the dead? yet fear not, for my Lord Jesus Christ hath compassion on thee and pitieth thee of his goodness.

And he went and opened the sepulchre, but found not the apostle there, for one of the brethren had stolen him away and taken him unto Mesopotamia; but from that place where the bones of the apostle had lain Misdaeus took dust and put it about his son's neck, saying: I believe on thee, Jesu Christ, now that he hath left me which troubleth men and opposeth them lest they should see thee. And when he had hung it upon his son, the lad became whole.

Misdaeus the king therefore was also gathered among the brethren, and bowed his head under the hands of Siphor the priest; and Siphor said unto the brethren: Pray ye for Misdaeus the king, that he may obtain mercy of Jesus Christ, and that he may no more remember evil against him. They all therefore, with one accord rejoicing, made prayer for him; and the Lord that loveth men, the King of Kings and Lord of lords, granted Misdaeus also to have hope in him; and he was gathered with the multitude of them that had believed in Christ, glorifying the Father and the Son and the Holy Ghost, whose is power and adoration, now and for ever and world without end.

Amen.

[U (and Syr.) ends:

The acts of Judas Thomas the apostle are completed, which he did in India, fulfilling the commandment of him that sent him. Unto whom be glory, world without end. Amen.]

THE BOOK OF THOMAS THE CONTENDER

John D. Turner (translator)

THE BOOK OF
THOMAS THE CONTENDER

The secret words that the savior spoke to Judas Thomas which I, even I, Mathaias, wrote down, while I was walking, listening to them speak with one another.

The savior said, "Brother Thomas while you have time in the world, listen to me, and I will reveal to you the things you have pondered in your mind.

"Now, since it has been said that you are my twin and true companion, examine yourself, and learn who you are, in what way you exist, and how you will come to be. Since you will be called my brother, it is not fitting that you be ignorant of yourself. And I know that you have understood, because you had already understood that I am the knowledge of the truth. So while you accompany me, although you are uncomprehending, you have (in fact) already come to know, and you will be called 'the one who knows himself'. For he who has not known himself has known nothing, but he who has known himself has at the same time already achieved knowledge about the depth of the all. So then, you, my brother Thomas, have beheld what is obscure to men, that is, what they ignorantly stumble against."

Now Thomas said to the lord, "Therefore I beg you to tell me what I ask you before your ascension, and when I hear from you about the hidden things, then I can speak about them. And it is obvious to me that the truth is difficult to perform before men."

The savior answered, saying, "If the things that are visible to you are obscure to you, how can you hear about the things that are not visible? If the deeds of the truth that are visible in the world are difficult for you to perform, how indeed, then, shall you perform those that pertain to the exalted height and to the pleroma which are not visible? And how shall you be called 'laborers'? In this respect you are apprentices, and have not yet received the height of perfection."

Now Thomas answered and said to the savior, "Tell us about these things that you say are not visible, but are hidden from us."

The savior said, "All bodies [...] the beasts are begotten [...] it is evident like [...] this, too, those that are above [...] things that are visible, but they are visible in their own root, and it is their fruit that nourishes them. But these visible bodies survive by devouring creatures similar to them with the result that the bodies change. Now that which changes will decay and perish, and has no hope of life from then on, since that body is bestial. So just as the body of the beasts perishes, so also will these formations perish. Do they not derive from intercourse like that of the beasts? If it, too derives from intercourse, how will it beget anything different from beasts? So, therefore, you are babes until you become perfect."

And Thomas answered, "Therefore I say to you, lord, that those who speak about things that are invisible and difficult to explain are like those who shoot their arrows at a target at night. To be sure, they shoot their arrows as anyone would - since they shoot at the target - but it is not visible. Yet when the light comes forth and hides the darkness, then the work of each will appear. And you, our light, enlighten, O lord."

Jesus said, "It is in light that light exists."

Thomas, spoke, saying, "Lord, why does this visible light that shines on behalf of men rise and set?"

The savior said, "O blessed Thomas, of course this visible light shines on your behalf - not in order that you remain here, but rather that you might come forth - and whenever all the elect abandon bestiality, then this light will withdraw up to its essence, and its essence will welcome it, since it is a good servant."

Then the savior continued and said, "O unsearchable love of the light! O bitterness of the fire that blazes in the bodies of men and in their marrow, kindling in them night and day, and burning the limbs of men and making their minds become drunk and their souls become deranged [...] them within males and females [...] night and moving them, [...] secretly and visibly. For the males move [...] upon the females and the females upon the males. Therefore it is said, "Everyone who seeks the truth from true wisdom will make himself wings so as to fly, fleeing the lust that scorches the spirits of men." And he will make himself wings to flee every visible spirit."

And Thomas answered, saying, "Lord, this is exactly what I am asking you about, since I have understood that you are the one who is beneficial to us, as you say."

Again the savior answered and said, "Therefore it is necessary for us to speak to you, since this is the doctrine of the perfect. If, now, you desire to become perfect, you shall observe these things; if not, your name is 'Ignorant', since it is impossible for an intelligent man to dwell with a fool, for the intelligent man is perfect in all wisdom. To the fool, however, the good and bad are the same - indeed the wise man will be nourished by the truth and (Ps. 1:3) "will be like a tree growing by the meandering stream" - seeing that there are some who, although having wings, rush upon the visible things, things that are far from the truth. For that which guides them, the fire, will give them an illusion of truth, and will shine on them with a perishable beauty, and it will imprison them in a dark sweetness and captivate them with fragrant pleasure. And it will blind them with insatiable lust and burn their souls and become for them like a stake stuck in their heart which they can never dislodge. And like a bit in the mouth, it leads them according to its own desire. And it has fettered them with its chains and bound all their limbs with the bitterness of the bondage of lust for those visible things that will decay and change and swerve by impulse. They have always been attracted downwards; as they are killed, they are assimilated to all the beasts of the perishable realm."

Thomas answered and said, "It is obvious and has been said, 'Many are [...] those who do not know [...] soul.'"

And the savior answered, saying, "Blessed is the wise man who sought after the truth, and when he found it, he rested upon it forever and was unafraid of those who wanted to disturb him."

Thomas answered and said, "It is beneficial for us, lord, to rest among our own?"

The savior said, "Yes, it is useful. And it is good for you, since things visible among men will dissolve - for the vessel of their flesh will dissolve, and when it is brought to naught it will come to be among visible things, among things that are seen. And then the fire which they see gives them pain on account of love for the faith they formerly possessed. They will be gathered back to that which is visible. Moreover, those who have sight among things that are not visible, without the first love they will perish in the concern for this life and the scorching of the fire. Only a little while longer, and that which is visible will dissolve; then shapeless shades will emerge, and in the midst of tombs they will forever dwell upon the corpses in pain and corruption of soul."

Thomas answered and said, "What have we to say in the face of these things? What shall we say to blind men? What doctrine should we express to these miserable mortals who say, "We came to do good and not curse," and yet claim, "Had we not been begotten in the flesh, we would not have known iniquity"?"

The savior said, "Truly, as for those, do not esteem them as men, but regard them as beasts, for just as beasts devour one another, so also men of this sort devour one another. On the contrary, they are deprived of the kingdom since they love the sweetness of the fire and are servants of death and rush to the works of corruption. They fulfill the lust of their fathers. They will be thrown down to the abyss and be afflicted by the torment of the bitterness of their evil nature. For they will be scourged so as to make them rush backwards, whither they do not know, and they will recede from their limbs not patiently, but with despair. And they rejoice over [...] madness and derangement [...] They pursue this derangement without realizing their madness, thinking that they are wise. They [...] their body [...] Their mind is directed to their own selves, for their thought is occupied with their deeds. But it is the fire that will burn them."

And Thomas answered and said, "Lord, what will the one thrown down to them do? For I am most anxious about them; many are those who fight them."

The savior answered and said, "What is your own opinion?"

Judas - the one called Thomas - said, "It is you, lord, whom it befits to speak, and me to listen."

The savior replied, "Listen to what I am going to tell you and believe in the truth. That which sows and that which is sown will dissolve in the fire - within the fire and the water - and they will hide in tombs of darkness. And after a long time they shall show forth the fruit of the evil trees, being punished, being slain in the mouth of beasts and men at the instigation of the rains and winds and air and the light that shines above."

Thomas replied, "You have certainly persuaded us, lord. We realize in our heart, and it is obvious, that this is so, and that your word is sufficient. But these words that you speak to us are ridiculous and contemptible to the world since they are misunderstood. So how can we go preach them, since we are not esteemed in the world?"

The savior answered and said, "Truly I tell you that he who will listen to your word and turn away his face or sneer at it or smirk at these things, truly I tell you that he will be handed over to the ruler above who rules over all the powers as their king, and he will turn that one around and cast him from heaven down to the abyss, and he will be imprisoned in a narrow dark place. Moreover, he can neither turn nor move on account of the great depth of Tartaros and the heavy bitterness of Hades that is steadfast [...] them to it [...] they will not forgive [...] pursue you. They will hand [...] over to [...] angel Tartarouchos [...] fire pursuing them [...]

fiery scourges that cast a shower of sparks into the face of the one who is pursued. If he flees westward, he finds the fire. If he turns southward, he finds it there as well. If he turns northward, the threat of seething fire meets him again. Nor does he find the way to the east so as to flee there and be saved, for he did not find it in the day he was in the body, so that he might find it in the day of judgment."

Then the savior continued, saying, "Woe to you, godless ones, who have no hope, who rely on things that will not happen!

"Woe to you who hope in the flesh and in the prison that will perish! How long will you be oblivious? And how long will you suppose that the imperishables will perish too? Your hope is set upon the world, and your god is this life! You are corrupting your souls!

"Woe to you within the fire that burns in you, for it is insatiable!

"Woe to you because of the wheel that turns in your minds!

"Woe to you within the grip of the burning that is in you, for it will devour your flesh openly and rend your souls secretly, and prepare you for your companions!

"Woe to you, captives, for you are bound in caverns! You laugh! In mad laughter you rejoice! You neither realize your perdition, nor do you reflect on your circumstances, nor have you understood that you dwell in darkness and death! On the contrary, you are drunk with the fire and full of bitterness. Your mind is deranged on account of the burning that is in you, and sweet to you are the poison and the blows of your enemies! And the darkness rose for you like the light, for you surrendered your freedom for servitude! You darkened your hearts and surrendered your thoughts to folly, and you filled your thoughts with the smoke of the fire that is in you! And your light has hidden in the cloud of [...] and the garment that is put upon you, you [...]. And you were seized by the hope that does not exist. And whom is it you have believed? Do you not know that you all dwell among those who that [...] you as though you [...]. You baptized your souls in the water of darkness ! You walked by your own whims!

"Woe to you who dwell in error, heedless that the light of the sun which judges and looks down upon the all will circle around all things so as to enslave the enemies. You do not even notice the moon, how by night and day it looks down, looking at the bodies of your slaughters!

"Woe to you who love intimacy with womankind and polluted intercourse with them! Woe to you in the grip of the powers of your body, for they will afflict you! Woe to you in the grip of the forces of the evil demons! Woe to you who beguile your limbs with fire! Who is it that will rain a refreshing dew on you to extinguish the mass of fire from you along with your burning? Who is it that will cause the sun to shine upon you to disperse the darkness in you and hide the darkness and polluted water?

"The sun and the moon will give a fragrance to you together with the air and the spirit and the earth and the water. For if the sun does not shine upon these bodies, they will wither and perish just like weeds or grass. If the sun shines on them, they prevail and choke the grapevine; but if the grapevine prevails and shades those weeds and all the other brush growing alongside, and spreads and flourishes, it alone inherits the land in which it grows; and every place it has shaded it dominates. And when it grows up, it dominates all the land and is bountiful for its master, and it pleases him even more, for he would have suffered great pains on account of these plants until he uprooted them. But the grapevine alone removed them and choked them, and they died and became like the soil."

Then Jesus continued and said to them, "Woe to you, for you did not receive the doctrine, and those who are [...] will labor at preaching [...]. And you are rushing into [...] will send them down [...] you kill them daily in order that they might rise from death.

"Blessed are you who have prior knowledge of the stumbling blocks and who flee alien things.

"Blessed are you who are reviled and not esteemed on account of the love their lord has for them.

"Blessed are you who weep and are oppressed by those without hope, for you will be released from every bondage.

"Watch and pray that you not come to be in the flesh, but rather that you come forth from the bondage of the bitterness of this life. And as you pray, you will find rest, for you have left behind the suffering and the disgrace. For when you come forth from the sufferings and passions of the body, you will receive rest from the good one, and you will reign with the king, you joined with him and he with you, from now on, for ever and ever, Amen."

The Book of Thomas The Contender Writing To the Perfect.
Remember me also, my brethren, in your prayers:
Peace to the saints and those who are spiritual.

Parchment Books is committed to publishing high quality
Esoteric/Occult classic texts at a reasonable price.

With the premium on space in modern dwellings, we also strive - within the limits of good book design - to make our products as slender as possible, allowing more books to be fitted into a given bookshelf area.

Parchment Books is an imprint of Aziloth Books, which has established itself as a publisher boasting a diverse list of powerful, quality titles, including novels of flair and originality, and factual publications on controversial issues that have not found a home in the rather staid and politically-correct atmosphere of many publishing houses.

Titles Include:

Secret Doctrines of the Rosicrucians	Magus Incognito
Corpus Hermeticum	(trans. GRS Mead)
The Virgin of the World	Hermes Trismegistus
Raja Yoga	Yogi Ramacharaka
Theosophy	Rudolf Steiner
The Most Holy Trinosophia	St Germain
The Gospel of Thomas	Anonymous
Pistis Sophia	(trans. GRS Mead)
The Siugnature of All Things	Jacob Boehme

Obtainable at all good online and local bookstores. View Aziloth's full list at:

www.azilothbooks.com

We are a small, approachable company and would love to hear any of your comments and suggestions on our plans, products, or indeed on absolutely anything.   Aziloth is also interested in hearing from aspiring authors whom we might publish. We look forward to meeting you. Contact us at:

info@azilothbooks.com

CATHEDRAL CLASSICS

Parchment Book's sister imprint, Cathedral Classics hosts an array of classic literature, from ancient tomes to twentieth-century masterpieces, all of which deserve a place in your home. A small selection is detailed below:

Mary Shelley	*Frankenstein*
H G Wells	*The Time Machine; The Invisible Man*
Niccolo Machiavelli	*The Prince*
Omar Khayyam	*The Rubaiyat of Omar Khayyam*
Joseph Conrad	*Heart of Darkness; The Secret Agent*
Jane Austen	*Persuasion; Northanger Abbey*
Oscar Wilde	*The Picture of Dorian Gray*
Voltaire	*Candide*
Bulwer Lytton	*The Coming Race*
Arthur Conan Doyle	*The Adventures of Sherlock Holmes*
John Buchan	*The Thirty-Nine Steps*
Friedrich Nietzsche	*Beyond Good and Evil*
Henry James	*Washington Square*
Stephen Crane	*The Red Badge of Courage*
Ralph Waldo Emmerson	*Self-Reliance, and Other Essays, (series 1&2)*
Sun Tzu	*The Art of War*
Charles Dickens	*A Christmas Carol*
Fyodor Dostoyevsky	*The Gambler; The Double*
Virginia Wolf	*To the Lighthouse; Mrs Dalloway.*
Johann W Goethe	*The Sorrows of Young Werther*
Walt Whitman	*Leaves of Grass - 1855 edition*
Confucius	*Analects*
Anonymous	*Beowulf*
Anne Bronte	*Agnes Grey*
More	*Utopia*
Farid ud-Din Attar	*The Conference of Birds*

full list at: www.azilothbooks.com

Obtainable at all good online and local bookstores.

CPSIA information can be obtained at www.ICGtesting.com
Printed in the USA
LVOW05s1813081014

407873LV00028B/1084/P